Dishonoured

Sofia Hayat

Dishonoured

I dared to live my life the way I wanted ...
so my parents set out to have me killed
A TRUE STORY

JOHN BLAKE

Published by John Blake Publishing Ltd,
3 Bramber Court, 2 Bramber Road,
London W14 9PB, England

www.johnblakepublishing.co.uk

First published in hardback in 2008

ISBN: 978-1-84454-701-2

British Library Cataloguing-in-Publication Data:

A catalogue record for this book is available from the British Library.

Design by www.envydesign.co.uk

Printed in Great Britain by CPI Bookmarque, Croydon, CR0 4TD

1 3 5 7 9 10 8 6 4 2

Papers used by John Blake Publishing are natural, recyclable products
made from wood grown in sustainable forests. The manufacturing processes
conform to the environmental regulations of the country of origin.

Every attempt has been made to contact the relevant copyright-holders,
but some were unobtainable. We would be grateful if the appropriate
people could contact us.

This book is dedicated to the following people ...

To Daphne, my guardian angel, who loved me without question, for who I was, what I was and for what I was about to become,. I miss our little chats. You were the first person who knew me.

To Saira, my sister, for being a good friend. You have always been someone I could trust, despite the beliefs of many people in our culture. You have a beautiful family, whom I adore. Hunnah, Humza, Haaris and Hussain. Happy children, confidant and extremely loving. Thank you for your special hugs and kisses.

I want to thank all those people who gave me a hard time, because you only made me stronger.

To Federica, who has been one of my best friends and whom I love with all my heart for being there. Thanks for giving me the kind of friendship I missed out on in school, and for picking me up when I fall.

To Monah, my adopted sister, and Kamran, my adopted brother just because you care.

To Mamma, Pappa, Luca and Marianna for being the best family a girl could have.

To Pompeo, for believing in me, and loving me, and putting up with my spontaneous creative soul.

To Angela, for giving me the gift of playing the piano

To all those people out there who have had to fight for who they are, and for all those people who are in the situations that I have been in. Learn to love yourself and who you are, and BECOME.

To Emma, without whom this book would probably never have been written. Thank you.

Finally to my mother. I love you.

'Honour Crimes' definition

Human rights abuses committed against women – most often by male relative in the name of 'family honour'. These crimes include battery, torture, mutilation, rape, forced marriage, imprisonment within the home, and even murder. These crimes are intended to 'protect the family honour'.

CONTENTS

PROLOGUE

Subj: (no subject)
Date: 21/06/2006 10:44:37 GMT
From: XXXXXXXX
To: Sofiahayat@XXXXX

Hi Sofia,

Don't know if you remember me. I emailed you about a year ago for some advice and I'm emailing to let you know that you changed my life.

I'm 19 years old, and formerly I was living at home with my parents and brothers. I don't know if you remember, but my passion in life has always been to partake in the performing arts. I love singing, dancing, acting – all of it! My parents and brothers regularly used to abuse me physically and mentally for loving this. They took me out of college and forced me to stay at home locked in my room. I thought I could escape to university, but that was not only out of the question, it was inconceivable. My family made my life a living hell even to the point where I didn't want to live. I actually attempted to kill myself. I was regularly beaten. Once my father found a packet of cigarettes in my bag and he burnt me with the lighter, then lit a cig and burnt me with that too.

But I emailed you and that saved me. I'm not being melodramatic, but what you said inspired me so much and gave me the courage to strike out on my own. I ran away from home and went to the police. They helped me sort out accommodation and get my few things from my parents. I'm now working in a theatre troupe, taking singing lessons, living with my boyfriend and enjoying my life. I have the freedom to come and go as I want. I can pursue my interests without the stigma of being 'unIslamic' or a bad Pakistani girl.

Sofia, I just wanted to say thank you. I know it doesn't matter to you, as I am just another girl, but I have to express to you what your words meant to me. They showed me that no one has the right to stop me living my life. I owe you a lot and you really are my inspiration. Because of you I faced my adversity head on and went on to live again.

Thank you once again. Take care and lots of love,

Arissa

After I'd read the e-mail from Arissa (not her real name), I felt worried about her. I turned away from the laptop and tried to clear my mind by staring out of the study window. I've always loved the view from my secluded private study, because the sight of the tranquil and sprawling North Downs always calms me.

It was the beginning of a beautiful summer day. I watched the sun pushing its way through the black clouds that were bubbling up and then disappearing over the rolling Kent hillside. I smiled as it began warming the lush green lawns that lay at the foot of our five-bedroom country house. Our two dogs were frolicking together on the patio by the swimming pool, enjoying the first rays of sunlight. They had found a paper party plate that they were tossing into the air with their noses. I smiled some more.

I remembered the evening before, when Fabrizio, my fiancé, and I had entertained a few of our close friends with an intimate champagne BBQ around the pool to celebrate my second feature-film wrap. We sipped champagne cocktails and watched the sun set over the back of our house, and my body had tingled with excitement as I imagined the upcoming film premiere in Cannes. It was called *The Unforgettable* and I played the lead role.

It was the summer of 2006 and I was so content. I felt liberated, confident and loved. I'd come to terms with my horrific, painful and solitary childhood and had forgiven many of those who had harmed me. It had been a gruelling 30 years that had often been devoid of love and affection, but after finally embracing life in the way that I'd always wanted to I had found success and fulfilment: I'd become an established actress with a thriving personal life. As I languished in the love that I'd always deserved, my past couldn't have been further away. A knock at the door jolted me out of my reverie.

'Come in, Maria,' I said. Maria had been our housekeeper for the past few years. She still is, and I don't know what I'd do without her. She's kind and unassuming and always knows what needs to be done without being told. I'm so thankful that Maria has a place in our busy but thriving family.

'I need to iron whatever you wanted to wear for your film casting in town this afternoon,' she said.

I looked at Maria blankly and smiled, but I couldn't focus on the film casting, not after reading Arissa's email. 'Oh, I'm not sure. What do you think I should wear?' I asked her distractedly.

'What about your fitted white shirt and the tailored black Chanel suit?' she replied.

'Perfect,' I said nonchalantly.

Maria began hunting through the array of pretty, colourful dresses that hung in my wardrobe. She found the items of clothing then left the room, softly closing the door behind her. I was alone again and, although I knew that I had to get on, I couldn't concentrate on the film casting or anything else until I'd tried to reach out to Arissa in some way. Something about her email was bothering me.

On the surface, Arissa's words seemed compelling and upbeat because she'd followed the advice that I had emailed her six months earlier. But I knew that, beneath their happy resonance, Arissa felt fearful and guilty – after all, I had gone through exactly the same thing. When Arissa had first written to me, I had advised her to run away from home and call the police, as I had done a few years earlier. Because of my upbringing, I had believed that

I was committing a sin and, while I had obtained my physical freedom, I felt unable to set myself free mentally. I knew that Arissa would be experiencing the same thing. I desperately wanted her to start enjoying her life and not waste any more years, as I had done. Arissa's flight to freedom had only just begun and because of her innocence and naivety I knew that I needed to help her further.

I picked up my mobile, took a deep breath and dialled.

'Hi, Arissa. It's Sofia Hayat,' I said cheerily.

Arissa sounded shocked and excited to hear from me. 'I can't believe it's you,' she said.

We chatted for a bit and then she asked if she could come and see me sometime. 'I know you are busy and I know that it's a silly question, but it would be wonderful if we could meet,' she said nervously.

I agreed to meet her the following Wednesday afternoon. Arissa would come to London and I would meet her at the station.

'I'll take you for lunch somewhere nice,' I said before we said goodbye.

'Great!' she said, sounding excited. 'See you then.'

I felt relieved that I had called. I knew there was still a job to be done with Arissa. I'd done what I needed to and now I could concentrate on the day ahead.

I wandered over and sat down at my cluttered dressing table. I picked up the casting notes that had been sitting there all morning, glanced quickly through them, then began to prepare my hair and make-up. I set to work applying a thin layer of translucent foundation to my skin and a natural pink to my lips. When I'd finished I stared at my reflection in the mirror and felt pleased. My raven-coloured hair looked pretty because I'd swept it up into a neat chignon at the back of my head. Two vintage diamante clips held it in place and glittered together, cleverly matching my sparkling dark-brown eyes.

As I looked into the mirror, I thought of the incredible journey and transformation that I'd made in my life. I no longer felt ugly and I no longer felt the need to cover my face with thick, dark make-up. I could even wear my hair just as I chose to. What a different story it had been when I'd looked in the mirror as a young child. Back then I'd never felt feminine or beautiful because I'd always been told that I wasn't. What's more, my once big, hooked nose, oily hair and acne-riddled Asian skin had led to severe self-doubt and self-loathing.

When my femininity had tried to burst through all the restrictions that had been placed on me by my family it was quickly put back in its box by them and the lid firmly shut.

'You're clothes are ready, Sofia,' said Maria from behind the closed door.

'Thanks, I'll be down in a second,' I said, looking away from the mirror. I wrapped my silk dressing gown around my body and stood up. Before I left the study to get changed downstairs, I wondered what Arissa looked like. I hoped her school friends hadn't bullied her like mine had and that she hadn't been restricted and abused at home because of the beautiful and feminine woman she quite rightly wanted to become.

Arissa and I met the next Wednesday. She didn't look anything like I'd looked as a child. She was petite and pretty, with hazel, almond-shaped eyes and pale, sallow skin. She spoke in soft, dulcet tones and seemed like an angel. I remember sitting in a restaurant in Notting Hill, holding her tiny hand and being struck by her fragility. She wasn't so different from the girl I'd been when I fled my family home all those years ago. Yes, we'd both been punished for wanting to follow our dreams, and had escaped the very people that were supposed to keep us safe and love us. But Arissa seemed sensitive, timid and delicate, just as I had been all those years ago.

'I ran away after you emailed me,' Arissa said. 'I felt better when I escaped, but now I think that I've sinned against God. I feel guilty and fearful of the consequences. My family will hurt me now for sure.' She gripped my hand tightly as she spoke.

'But you're free now to follow your dreams, Arissa. You're a very brave young woman,' I told her. 'It doesn't say anywhere in the Koran that a person should kill or harm a member of their own family. Your family was harming you because of how they wrongly view our culture. They see themselves as upstanding people, as the pillars in our society, when they are really far from those things. But our culture doesn't want a woman to feel like this, and neither does God. The sad thing is that your parents unfortunately know no different. Their false beliefs are deeply ingrained within them.'

I paused and smiled at her. 'You need to keep in contact with the police and always keep my number with you,' I added.

We sat for a few moments in silence. I think Arissa understood and believed what I was saying but when she looked across at me, trying to smile, I knew she'd still face an immense struggle in her future. I was worried that Arissa wouldn't have the strength I'd had to follow her journey through and rid herself of her fear and guilt. I wanted to help her as much as I could and was relieved that I'd come to meet her.

After lunch, we walked to the road and I hailed a cab for her. I pressed a twenty-pound note into Arissa's hand and kissed her cheek.

'You take care and call me or the police if you ever need anything. Remember, you must never feel guilty and you must never fear anything. You're a human being and you deserve to be happy. I'm here for you always,' I said clearly as she climbed into the cab.

Arissa nodded and thanked me, but as the cab pulled away she turned to wave back at me and I saw that she wasn't smiling at all – her delicate face was blank and cold. My heart sank because I suspected that nothing and no one would really be able to comfort her, for Arissa believed that her family would find and harm her.

Over the next six months I thought about Arissa every day and prayed for her regularly. On New Year's Eve, I sent her a text message to wish her a Happy New Year – I knew how having just one person to turn to during those difficult moments really made a difference. But when I read the reply I was shocked.

'Arissa fell into a coma and died,' it read, and that was all.

I called her number as the panic rose in me. A woman answered.

'I'm a friend of Arissa's,' I said. 'What happened?'

There was a short pause. 'It's terrible,' began the woman nervously. 'Arissa was set upon by some youths in Moss Side and she died. I'm just taking calls. Please be mindful of her family and pray for them. They won't be at the funeral. They said that in their eyes Arissa was dead anyway.'

Before I had a chance to speak, the woman hung up.

My body froze, but after a few moments my mind began to race. Hearing that Arissa had come to such an end was so awful but, after thinking it over a little, my instincts told me that something wasn't right. I called directory enquiries and asked to be put through to Moss Side Police Station. There was no record of a crime against Arissa, and no record of any recent attack that fitted the description I gave them. The policeman suggested I tried other police stations. I thanked him and then spent the next hour calling every police station in and around Manchester, desperate to find out what had really happened to my friend. No one had any record of her death.

Later that night, I tried her mobile number again. The line was dead. To this day I still don't know where Arissa is or even if she's alive.

I often get emails from young Asian girls like Arissa who are desperate to find love, enjoy their femininity and their freedom. Many of them will never enjoy what they deserve because of their family's misconceptions about Asian culture. What's worse is the intense fear and guilt that is put into their beautiful, innocent hearts. Family members often resort to using violence so that their daughters are forever constrained behind four walls.

I have been violated, constrained and filled with fear and guilt. I have even faced the prospect of death at the hands of my very own family. Despite this, my incredible journey has taught me that our Asian culture is, at heart, a beautiful and free one, and that a woman's feminine power and freedom is as important as any man's. Many Asians still need to try to recognise these things, and it is up to my generation to instil a change for the better, instead of sweeping these matters under the carpet. I know so many Asians who on the surface seem to be devout but who, in reality, go out clubbing, have relationships and drink; all the things their parents forbid them from doing. If everyone could be a bit more open about it, I think there would be fewer problems between the older and the younger generations.

In this supposedly free-thinking day and age, I hope that we can all make a change. I hope that we can all release ourselves from the past for the sake of freedom in mind and body, and also for the sake of the progression of women's rights.

CHAPTER ONE

HONOUR

I was born on 6 December 1974 at Gravesend Hospital in Kent. It was a natural, unproblematic birth and I was my mother's second child. My elder sister Zarqa had arrived two years beforehand when my mother Surriya Qureishi and my father Zamarad were still living in Pakistan.

I think the seeds of unhappiness within our family unit were sown very early on because my mother was only a teenager when she fell prey to an arranged marriage. It upsets me to think that I wasn't born out of love, but rather out of fear and force. Despite this, my mother bore my father six children.

My mother recently told me that she didn't really want to marry my dad. 'I didn't think I could ever really love him because he was always so aggressive and cold to me,' she said, her face expressionless. 'His family also frightened me, but when I was 19 my family pushed me into marrying him because your father's cousin went to school with my father. We were thought of as a good match, our parents arranged everything and that was that. I fell pregnant with Zarqa a year later.'

I often used to search my mother's eyes when she talked about her loveless marriage, yet all I saw was a calm acceptance of what was an unhealthy and purely practical arrangement. I was mistaken. Now, I know that my mother's eyes conceal a very different emotion: deep fear of ever shaming her family and of one of her own children ever shaming her.

In 1972, my father decided he wanted to make his fortune in Britain. At the time there was political unrest in Pakistan and he'd heard that the streets were paved with gold over here. 'Your father packed his belongings and promised me that we could join him later,' Mum told me. 'Many Asian men were being welcomed into Britain by the government at the time, but when your father arrived it wasn't as he'd expected it to be. Assimilation was tough and the hostility towards men like him was often frightening. In the end he settled in Gravesend in Kent but still found life here very hard. All he had were the clothes on his back and a five-pound note in his pocket. All he wanted to do was to give us some sort of a decent life. And he tried.'

Back then, Gravesend was a town where a lot of Asians chose to settle because it was near the coast and near London. There were many factories springing up nearby and my father found work in one that made toilet paper. It must have been a tough time for Dad, but I remember that we always had plenty of free toilet paper in the house when I was little. It was the only thing I remember enjoying in abundance!

Dad could just about get by on his £18 a week. But he had to stretch his small wage even further when my mother and baby Zarqa finally joined him a year later. They had to move into a larger rented room because of the baby, but it was still pretty grim. Their new home was another tiny box room in a sparse and dirty four-bedroom house. Mum told me how they lived with four other Asian couples, but that she always made sure that everyone was as comfortable as possible. She had a baby girl to keep fed and clean, but was determined to make sure they survived.

'We had to share the same cramped and unhygienic bathroom and kitchen with everyone, but your father worked even harder for us until we managed to move to a nicer room in another shared house on Denton Road. That is where you actually spent the first few weeks of your life, Sofia,' she said.

I was too young to remember that poverty-stricken beginning, but the picture I have from my mother is of a life of extreme hardship. The start of her new life here was drenched in so much fear. She was fearful of how the Asian community viewed her, and she felt threatened by the unfamiliar British community around her.

Her fear only increased on the day that I was born. After my mother had carried me home from Gravesend Hospital, my father came back from the registry office and told her bluntly that he had signed my birth certificate and changed my surname from Sofia Hayat-Khan to Sofia Hayat.

'I want Sofia to have as much chance as anyone else has when she applies for jobs or goes to school,' he said, brushing his thin, wiry moustache in the cracked mirror on the grimy bedroom wall. 'If she has the surname "Khan" she won't be given the same opportunities in her life as everyone else gets. I don't want Sofia to be discriminated against because of her Pakistani surname.'

Up until that evening, my mum had felt safe in their tiny room on Denton Road. Although my father was a dominating character, his presence was a comfort to her, as was the fact that there were other Asian families living in the rooms next door.

Suddenly, everything changed.

'I remember cradling you as I sat on the rickety wooden bed,' recalled Mum. 'I wrapped you up tightly in an old cotton blanket and shivered at your father's aggressive, stern words. I wondered if we were in trouble living there. I asked him what he meant and why he talked about discrimination. But all he said was that crying wasn't going to help anything and that he'd done the right thing.'

Eventually, the truth came out. Dad told her that he'd heard other Asian children in the area had been discriminated against because of their surnames and because of the colour of their skin. He also warned her about the National Front.

Mum didn't feel safe any more, and soon her sense of security would be challenged even further by my father's actions. Sadly, his eye had started to wander. There was a girl in another room in the house who was the same age as Mum, and my father started to see her. Mum was told to keep out of the way, but she could not turn a blind eye.

'I had to confront him about it,' said Mum. 'It took a lot for me to do it because normally in our culture the wife should keep quiet and continue to obey. If she doesn't she will always get into trouble. I couldn't keep quiet, though, because I felt he'd broken my trust. It was such an insult because I hadn't wanted to wed him in the first place. I suffered the consequences though.'

In the end, my mother stayed with my father because she

felt that she had no choice and she had no one else to turn to. If Mum had sought help within the Asian community, she assumed that her family's reputation would have been tarnished. A divorce would have dishonoured her family in Pakistan; their friends in Gravesend would have banished her and our family would have been shamed. Mum still believes that she never really had a choice.

My parents went on to have more children despite my father's infidelity. My mother gave him two more girls and two boys, one year after another. We were all given two names, our Christian names and a nickname. I was nicknamed Rosy. We call my sister Bubble, but her real name is Saira, and my other sister is called Tahira and Bushra respectively. My brother Abdul Wajid is called Boogie, my other brother Abdul Majid is called Papoo and my older sister Zarqa is called Rani.

To this day, we're all very proud of our names, roots and heritage as real British Asians, but I will always wish that I could have had the name that was supposed to rightfully be mine. More than this, though, I wish that my parents had loved one another and that 'honour' – 'Izaat' as we called it – hadn't held our family together falsely and then wrecked it in the end. Though, like my mother, growing up I knew no different. As a child I respected and abided by our honour as best I could. I knew full well that if I didn't I'd also be harmed just like my mother. Living in fear is a terrible thing. It takes immense courage to confront it.

CHAPTER TWO

POVERTY AND PRAYERS

When I was three months old, my parents moved to a council house on Bentley Street. My father was earning a bit more money by this time because he was working for ever-increasing amounts of time, but things were still very tight for us. To help, my mother got a job during the day so that my father could work nights. It was tough, but they were soon bringing in £35 a week between them. Mum worked for companies where she'd clean alloy wheels, drill car parts together and operate large noisy machinery. They needed to clothe and feed their children.

Our new home was in a grey stone house that stood opposite a dark industrial car park. There were two bedrooms, a living room and kitchen, all of which were sparsely furnished. My mother had bought our main pieces of furniture from various second-hand shops in Gravesend and all the other bits and pieces had come from family friends. I remember our wooden bunk beds most of all. There were six of them, and all the children and my mother slept in them in one room. My father had his own room with a bed to himself.

As kids, we probably assumed that my parents' strange sleeping arrangement was because they were working different hours. It made sense to us, but in reality the reason they slept apart was very different.

'Your father and I were living separate lives by that point,' Mum told me. 'We didn't want to be in the same bedroom as one another. I was glad about it, though, because the separation enabled me to have some distance from your father. I didn't want to be near him.'

Mum must have felt so alone. Moving to Bentley Street should have felt like a brand-new start for her, but unfortunately her fear only increased because, on top of her domestic worries, our whole family then came face to face with something equally traumatic: racism. When we moved to the new flat, we'd unknowingly moved into the heart of racist England. Bentley Street was right in the centre of the National Front area.

'We were in the thick of a racist war zone,' said Mum. 'These violent men had a lot of power and were strongly anti-Asian, so it was really frightening for me having to protect my children from them.'

Mum wasn't aware of how tough it was going to be until she moved in. If she was scared of life at home with Dad, she was now scared for us to leave the house. 'Sometimes we weren't allowed to go into the centre of Gravesend for fear of being beaten by them. I'd take you down the street in your pram with your sister and notice gangs of men standing in doorways and on pavements just watching me.'

The Asian community warned people to be careful and it soon became clear that Mum didn't want her children to become assimilated into such a violent society – it was simply impossible. She made sure that we didn't integrate so that we didn't get caught up in any trouble. 'I knew which shops not to enter and which streets not to walk down,' she said with terror in her eyes.

Even though she describes a life of poverty and fear, when my mother talks about my early years I really can't remember feeling unhappy at that age. I do remember that my mother always counted the pennies and that she rarely spoke to my father, but it never really bothered me since I was too young to know different.

However, during Ramadan I remember that when other families gave us kids money – as is traditional during Ramadan – we always gave it back to my mother. She'd then give it to other kids in the community because we couldn't afford to do it any other way. I also remember that we hardly had any food. We'd live off eggs for breakfast and then have curry, rice, chapattis and tap water in the evenings. Even when we started going to school I remember that my mother always had to borrow money from friends just so we could have packed lunches like the other school kids. That we were unable to eat properly shows how difficult things were for us financially. But we all just made do.

I never minded that we always had to share clothes and toys. I enjoyed sharing anything with my siblings anyway, but I was always dressed in hand-me-downs and never had many toys of my own. Because of our culture, we wore an outfit known as Shalwaar Kameez – a typical, plain long top and matching trousers. At that age, wearing frayed hand-me-downs seemed fine. Everyone else that I knew in the community wore the same, so it never bothered me.

My favourite toy was my sister's Honey Monster. I don't know where it came from, but it was big, yellow and cuddly. Whenever I woke up at night, I'd sneak downstairs, carefully switch the fire on and play with it. The Honey Monster and the fire would always make me feel warm and comforted at night, until one day when he caught fire! I shrieked loudly and woke everyone up, but luckily the house didn't burn down!

I was happy, despite our poverty, and unaware of the external and internal aggression that was eating away at my poor mother. I was simply happy playing with my siblings, but I think our happiness as children was mostly down to my sister Zarqa.

Zarqa was the one who really brought us all up. She was a bright light in our lives and would happily occupy us as much as she could whenever my parents were busy working. I didn't notice that I wasn't getting any love and attention from them because Zarqa managed to fill the gap, for a while at least. She always made sure that there wasn't a dull moment and always gave us things to do. Zarqa was very regimented and conscientious about our religious education and chores. We always followed the same ritual.

'Wake up, Sofia, wake up,' I remember Zarqa saying every morning.

I'd be lying fast asleep under the warm brown blanket in my wooden bunk bed and the room was always pitch black when I opened my eyes. Because it was so early, it felt like the rest of the world was fast asleep, but I'd pull myself up and sleepily climb down the ladder that was attached to the front of my bunk bed. I'd then go to the bathroom and perform Wazoo, a cleansing ritual. I'd clean most of my face and arms, then my nose and behind my ears and finally my feet. After washing I'd fetch my prayer mat from the top of the cupboard in the bedroom and I'd crouch down to pray with my sisters and brothers before the sun rose. We always prayed facing Mecca and at that time I always prayed twice a day. I enjoyed thanking God for everyone else's success and praying for my family and the poor people around the world. Then I would pray for myself.

I relished those times on my prayer mat because it gave me purpose, inspiration and security, plus for a child it was fun. I loved being with my siblings and sharing those moments with them and I remember feeling happy that I had this amazing religion in my life. It also felt good because whenever I prayed I won my parents' approval, and at that age their approval mattered so much to me. Even if they never vocalised their feelings towards me, thinking that they loved me because I was good and respectful towards them and God was more than enough to make me feel content.

After prayers we would set to work cleaning. Because we couldn't afford to replace our broken vacuum-cleaner, we used to run around the house happily picking up bits of dirt from the floor. 'Whoever can find the most specks of dirt gets something special!' Zarqa would squeal as we charged around the living room, frantically searching for anything we could find before dashing up to Zarqa to show her how many crumbs we'd found. Then she would hug each of us warmly. Then it was time for breakfast, and once that was over we'd learn the Koran.

We always read the Koran in Arabic. My mother thought it was important for us to read the language – I never understood Arabic, but I learned how to read it. My parents promised us that, once we were in heaven, we would understand the true meaning of the Koran, which I found confusing as I wanted to understand it now. So, under Zarqa's watchful eye, that's exactly what we did. Looking back, I did learn a lot from my family's teaching of the Koran, plus I enhanced this knowledge by reading an English translation of it. I still live by many of its words. But I am careful not to distort it. For me – then and now – Islam is about peace and forgiveness and is an instruction and mantra that I will always follow in my own way.

I never felt any restriction back then because, as kids, we didn't have to cover up. Our femininity hadn't started to blossom, so there wasn't a need within me to want to nourish it. All we did was pray, fast and go to the mosque. I honoured and respected my family and our culture and, just like all the other kids in our community, I felt like I had a place.

When I got a bit older, I also began fasting. During Ramadan, the month of fasting, we got up before sunrise and prayed – and then we didn't eat or drink until sunset. As an adult, fasting really gives you strength of mind and enables you to empathise with those less fortunate than yourself. If you go about your daily business and feel thirsty or see someone eating in the street, it makes you appreciate how lucky you really are. It's truly humbling. As a child, though, it was particularly difficult when the weather was warm because I always felt thirsty and wanted a drink of water – especially if we'd had PE at school.

Eid is a joyous Muslim festival which marks the end of Ramadan. Typically, Muslims wake up on the morning of Eid, have a small breakfast, dress in new clothes and then attend special Eid prayers at the Mosque. We also have to pay 'Zakat', or charity, which is a percentage of your wages for the year, or a food donation.

On this day, Muslims embrace each other in the spirit of peace, forgiveness, moral victory and brotherhood. We thank God for his help and for giving us the strength to exercise self-control during the period of fasting.

I carried on praying even when I finally started at a local mixed school. I began my first term at Cecil Road School when I four years old. Most of the kids in my class were from my own community and I fitted in easily. There was an indoor pool and two playgrounds, and I loved the space during the daytimes – up until then I'd been cooped up at home in the small lhouse. I also liked it at Cecil Road because my brother went to the nursery next door. It was great to watch him from the school fence as he played happily at break times on the yellow plastic swings and the slide.

The main happiness that I discovered at Cecil Road was performing. I acted in my first school play when I was six and remember how fantastic it had felt standing on stage, happily narrating in front of all the other kids. Funnily enough, I'd been in a car accident before the play, and because I'd been injured I had these awful scabs all over my face. It was a hit-and-run, and I had landed on my face. The teachers and my parents didn't want me to perform, but I was determined to go on stage, and persisted until they gave in.

I can still remember one line, when I had to look at the baubles on the Christmas tree and say, 'The balls sparkled on the tree at Christmas.' But because my lips had so many scabs on them, it came out as, 'The galls karkled on the tree at Chrissas.' Looking back, I must have looked like something out of a horror film! When the play was over, though, the teachers showered me with praise.

That play was a defining point in my life. It was probably the first time I felt a creative spirit within me. Being complimented by an adult was such a positive feeling, but the negative side was that such praise highlighted a gap in my life at home. Zarqa had always tried her best to love, care for and praise me, but she wasn't an adult and she wasn't my mother. My mother had never praised me like my teachers had done after my performance. She'd never hugged me like they'd hugged me either. The teachers had lavished this alien attention on me, and in its absence at home I began to crave it more and more.

CHAPTER THREE
THE CORNER SHOP

When I was seven, we moved to a two-bedroom flat above a corner shop in Old Road West. My father had saved enough for a mortgage and thought that he could make more money there running his own business. The flat was just as small as the house on Bentley Street but, because we'd also bought the corner shop, it felt like we had more living space. And, with eight of us living there, we needed it. Even so, on a recent visit I realised just how small it really was. It was so different from how I remembered it. I felt sad, though, when I looked around the tiny box rooms and down on to the two-metre-wide concrete back yard. I wouldn't put more than two people in there nowadays!

Our new home was still in the National Front area. This worried my mother, but my parents just made sure that we kept ourselves to ourselves. Although we were all going to school, where we had white friends, outside of school she continued to make sure that we never mixed with the white British locals.

I vividly remember the day that we moved into the flat. We packed up our belongings into plastic shopping bags and traipsed down the street to Old West Road. When we arrived outside the shop, we walked round the back and into the small square-shaped concrete yard. Because we had to wait for the furniture to arrive we all stood in the yard chatting. There were a few chickens clucking about. They looked happy enough, and I remember thinking that I wanted to make friends with them. I started chasing them around on the concrete, and before long was really enjoying my new little playmates and was even planning what names to give them.

'We need to kill them so don't get too close,' my father said suddenly.

I stopped in my tracks and shuddered. 'But they're lovely chickens, Dad. I'm making friends with them. I'll look after them properly.' His words had made me feel so upset.

'We need them for food, Sofia. Don't be silly.'

And that was that. I always obeyed and respected my father's wishes, so I knew that mentioning taking care of the chickens again certainly wasn't an option. That episode with the chickens is my first memory of my father aggressively clamping down on anything fun in my life.

Once the furniture was in, we were finally allowed to go upstairs. I noticed straight away that the flat was small, cramped and ugly. But I was thankful that downstairs in the little corner shop there would be plenty of people to chat to, and sweets and biscuits galore!

Because I ended up hating that flat, the corner shop soon became my little haven. I was so happy downstairs, mainly because, like at school, I could breathe and enjoy myself in the space. I loved all the different smells that wafted in and out of the shop when it was summer and the door would be propped open with two tins of baked beans. I'd never seen so many colourful sweets, tasty chocolates and packets of scrumptious crisps and biscuits. I always remember listening out for the sound of the bell above the door. When it chimed, I knew that a customer had gone inside. I'd dart downstairs, sneak into the shop and hide in one of the aisles to see who'd come in and find out what they were buying. If my father was busy serving another customer, sometimes I'd say 'hi' to customers without Dad noticing. I'd even pretend that it was my little shop, that the customers were my best friends and that they'd come especially to see me. Although I was only six or seven years old, I loved my new little fantasy world because it took me away from the dull, cramped flat upstairs.

My fondest memory was when my brother Boogie had his first birthday and we hired a video camera for the weekend. It was a real treat for us – business had been going well in the corner shop, so Dad allowed us to hire it.

'Can't you film me?' I begged, hoping that they'd film me all day. 'I can act and sing for you. Boogie can't do what I can, he's a baby, so please film me!' I twirled around and danced as best as I could, making everyone else laugh. That was my first time in front of the lens and I remember just wanting to do more.

At that point, I lived with a growing feeling of being unloved by my parents, but overall I was still fairly happy being cared for by Zarqa and escaping to the shop whenever I needed to. We still had our routine – Zarqa would get us up at sunrise and then put us to bed by 9pm. We'd pray together, go to school, and that was good enough for me.

But life began to change. After a year or so, my father started seeing other women again. There was a girl who came to help out in the shop (let's call her Carol). Carol was only 16 years old and wore skinny jeans and had long, straight, dark hair. She'd wear it to the side and I remember that whenever she'd look up through her fringe she looked just like Princess Diana. I'll never know what she saw in my father, but they definitely had something going on.

Once or twice, Carol would help out in the corner shop. Because I loved hiding away in my little world downstairs, I probably saw more than I should have seen. I'd often spot my father laughing and flirting with Carol at the back of the shop. I'd never seen my father kiss or laugh with another woman so naturally I felt confused.

My confusion soon turned to anger at my father for this show of affection towards another woman. Although I was still young, by this time I had grasped that he was betraying my mother, but I was not old enough to understand why. My mother was beautiful and timid, with big Bambi-like eyes and I couldn't understand why my father was giving attention and showing kindness to another woman when it was my mum who did everything for him. Plus, he'd never shown affection towards me. If anything he'd become slightly aggressive towards me. At this point I'd also begun to feel isolated since I couldn't tell my siblings or my mother what I'd seen. I'd already started to feel like I was the odd one out in the family anyway. My two brothers were best friends and so were my younger sisters, so I felt like I didn't have a friend in them. Zarqa was at the helm obviously, but because she was more of a mother figure to me she didn't come into the picture.

I later found out that my mother knew what was going

on between my dad and Carol anyway. 'I felt angry again,' Mum confessed. 'But I couldn't confront him or tell anyone as it would've shamed us all.'

Amidst all this turmoil, and with growing feelings of isolation, restriction and neglect, I began spending more and more time alone. It seemed safer that way. In my secure and lonely space I took comfort knowing that my cheating, controlling father and my distant siblings couldn't really let me down. I began to spend more and more time daydreaming. I'd either retreat downstairs to the corner shop where my fantasy world would take over, or I'd climb on to my wooden bunk bed where I'd daydream away at the window while looking out on to the street below.

In the end, my daydreaming started to challenge the reality of a dull, restricted and loveless childhood. All I had were those idyllic moments on my bunk bed when my imagination could run wild and take me away from it all. I'd sit at the window and daydream about what it would be like to feel love and have someone kiss me, or I'd watch the two boys who lived next door happily kicking their football around, or gaze at the girl in the pretty lemon-yellow dress at number 17 laughing at them on the pavement. I'd imagine myself down on the street wearing a pink gingham dress, my hair in bows, playing happily and freely with the other children. But the stark reality of my existence was that I couldn't ever join in. I wasn't allowed to play in the street or wear colourful dresses. I was also restricted in what I could watch on the television, couldn't listen to music or even read magazines. When I was eight years old I knew that I wasn't free and I hated it.

My parents obviously sensed a change in their once-happy, rule-abiding daughter. They noticed that I'd become distracted and quiet and that I was retreating more and more into my little fantasy world. Perhaps they saw that I was beginning to want a taste of the outside world that they feared, and this led to their tightening up their rules even more.

It was over an Asian boy called Georgie that my father really lost his temper with me. Georgie lived a few minutes' drive away and I was normally allowed to spend time with him whenever my parents visited his parents. I loved going over to play with him because Georgie had fire engines and action men. Even though they were boys' toys, being able to touch and look at them always made me feel happy because toys were so sparse at home. He also lived in a proper family house, which reminded me of the ones in Bollywood films. One Saturday morning I asked my parents if I could go with them to Georgie's.

'No,' said Mum. 'You need to do your chores and clean up today. There's a lot to be done in the shop too. You also need to pray properly. You didn't pray enough last night so you need to do extra today.'

I was led to believe that she was saying all this for my own good and I suppose deep down I realised that she was.

Mum wandered off down into the shop to tell my father to leave me behind. I remember going straight to my room and sitting on my bed, upset and frustrated. To make matters worse, when I looked out of the window I saw my father driving off with my sisters and brothers. I was so angry that I'd been left behind that in the end I decided to walk there all on my own. It would be my first rebellion, albeit a small one. But that first rebellion brought some serious consequences.

I put my coat on and left the flat. I thought I knew

exactly which roads to walk down to get to Georgie's house and, although I knew that it was a dangerous journey, I didn't care if anyone stopped me or saw me. All I wanted was to be with Georgie and to be able to play with his toys just like my brothers and sisters were able to. The trouble was that I ended up getting completely lost and wandering up the busy motorway on my own. I felt frightened as I stood alone on the hard shoulder watching the cars speeding past me. I had no idea where I was, and was starting to panic. Just at the point where I didn't know what to do next, I saw my father's car coming towards me on the hard shoulder. I was so relieved that he'd come and found me. Little did I know that all hell was about to break loose.

'You've disobeyed me, Sofia,' shouted my father through the car window as he pulled into the hard shoulder.

I was quivering with fear from the traffic as he picked me up and pushed me into the back of the car. I remember him shouting at me all the way home, and by the time we got back I was crying uncontrollably.

'If you ever disobey me again then you'll be punished,' he snarled as he pulled me out of the car and dragged me up the metal staircase.

Once we were inside the flat, my father seemed to go berserk. His eyes were red and burning with anger as he shouted at me and called me all the names under the sun. When he had finished scolding me, he left the room and, after a few minutes, I picked myself up and crawled up to the bedroom and hid under my bunk bed. I stayed there for four hours.

Although the transition between feeling happy with life and then sad happened really quickly, out of all the things that were going on, it was my father's behaviour that really shocked me. His anger came like a bolt from the blue – sometimes it was when I'd misbehaved over small things and at other times, when I was beginning to deliberately test his boundaries just as any child might, I half-expected a reaction.

I was only allowed chocolate as a special treat, about once a week. Sometimes, I would steal some from the shop and get caught by my father.

'Sofia, what's in your mouth?' Dad would shout when he'd catch me in the shop hiding a mouthful of Kit Kat.

'I was hungry, Dad,' I'd reply, knowing full well that what I'd done was strictly forbidden. But before I could swallow the Kit Kat or whatever else I'd taken from off the sweet shelf, my father would have sent me out into the small courtyard where I'd have to stand alone for hours and miss the evening meal.

While my father's attitude towards me worsened, we also encountered further problems with the National Front. The worst day I remember was when my mother received a distraught phone call from a friend of hers warning her that there was going to be a march through the streets. Mum became pretty hysterical.

I remember my mother screaming at us, 'They're going to smash up all the Asian shops. We need to leave now, children. They're coming to harm us and smash up the shop,' she shrieked as she ran around the flat packing anything she could find into bags.

I was scared stiff and ran up to Zarqa who tried to calm me down.

'Don't worry, Sofia,' Zarqa said. 'We'll leave now. It'll be fine if we go in time. Go and put your coat on.' Then she tried to pacify my mother.

But my mother couldn't be placated. Just as we were about to leave the flat she ran round to a neighbour's house to see if she could get some help. My mother was desperate to save the shop so when she returned she had our neighbour Phyllis, who was white, in tow.

'Phyllis is going to stand in the shop so they think she owns it. We can all then just hide out in the back yard,' stammered Mum, her face white with fear.

'What if they see us?' I asked Zarqa as we left the flat.

'They won't,' she said, calm as ever.

We crept fearfully down the metal staircase and huddled in silence in the back yard. The chickens clucked happily around us. Soon we heard the angry men marching down our street. Luckily they went straight past the shop. An hour later, Phyllis gave us the all-clear and we went back upstairs.

Phyllis soon began working in the shop full-time because my parents were so worried that the National Front might attack us if they came back without warning. I felt like Phyllis had saved our lives that day, but I also felt angry that these people had ruined my playtime in the corner shop. From then on, I didn't want to go back round into the corner shop any more because I thought that I might get hurt. My haven, my place of happiness, had been destroyed.

After that day we heard regularly how other Asians had been beaten and hurt or had their house and shop windows smashed. Eventually, we had our own run-in with the National Front to tell people about. It happened one day while we were enjoying tea in the street. Some National Front men spotted us and set upon us. It was terrifying as I saw them approaching, but it was too late to get away. I remember this man's face snarling at me, and then he started calling me names.

'F***ing Pakis, go back to where you came from.'

I was petrified. Then he smashed my teacup to the ground and stamped my piece of cake into the pavement. They smashed more cake in our faces and turned over our chairs and table in the road. And then it was over.

That incident was my first real brush with racism, and the violence of it left me so fearful. I'd just turned nine years old and I remember wishing that I was white because back then I assumed being white led to safety, freedom and happiness. Suddenly, having a darker skin colour felt like a curse. It seemed skanky and bad to be Asian and it felt like I was being punished for it.

'Can't I change my skin colour, Mum?' I'd beg her whenever I felt threatened by the National Front. 'Why am I different?'

But my mother never replied. Because I never got an answer from her, I assumed she didn't want to help or protect me. I realise now that she had her own battles with my father and with the racists and couldn't answer the questions I had.

Despite the aggression from my father and from the National Front, I still managed to find a small amount of happiness in my mind. If ever I felt afraid or sad, I'd stay upstairs on my bed and write songs about men, women and love. I was desperate to find beauty around me, and I did – in my imagination. Whether it was a picture that I'd created in my mind or a song that I'd written on my battered school notepad, I always found what I needed to take my mind somewhere else. It was daydream stuff that felt colourful and warm and so unlike the stark reality of everyday life at home.

From a young age, I came to believe that being self-contained was the way for me to be happy. I didn't want to feel isolated, beaten, unloved or a victim of racism. In order to escape all the negative things that had crept into my once happy life, I withdrew into my own world. I had to depend on myself. I had to emotionally support and rely on myself for happiness. I had to be my own mother, my own father and my own friend.

And that process had begun when I was eight years old.

CHAPTER FOUR
THE UNCLE

When I was ten, we moved again. Our new house on Northcote Road would be my last proper family home. It was an end-of-terrace, four-bedroom place, and had a rickety old railway track at the foot of a lovely unkempt and wild garden.

It was great having more space inside, but what I truly loved was having the garden to wander around in on my own. It made a nice change from sitting on my wooden bunk bed and staring out of a window at a world that I couldn't be a part of. 'Where's that Sofia now?' I remember hearing my mother shouting most mornings when I'd wandered off on my own. 'It's time to go to school, Sofia. Where are you? Zarqa, is she lying on her bed looking out of the window daydreaming again?'

I would have rushed through my chores and would be standing at the end of the garden, or wandering around, poking about in the shrubs and bushes looking for animals and bugs.

In the summer, I loved waking up at sunrise and spending my mornings in the garden. After I'd prayed, I'd wolf down a piece of toast, head towards the train track, and wait patiently for the train to pass by. Around 7.30am, I'd hear the train chuffing away in the distance. When it went past me I'd watch the passengers on their way to work with their heads buried in their morning newspapers. Sometimes I spotted school kids pressing their noses against the misty windows and smiled up at them. Sometimes they smiled back and then we'd wave to each other. It made me feel so happy. If ever I was feeling lonely or had been upset by my father I'd wish that the train would stop so that I could clamber on board and disappear to wherever they were going.

As well as spending time alone at home, I also started to withdraw more at school. It wasn't because I didn't want to study hard or achieve good grades there, or because I didn't want to mix with other kids, but because I'd started to be bullied. By this time I'd left the nice, friendly Cecil Road School and was at another local school called St Mary's. My class was predominantly white, although there were Asians in the school.

The bullying started mainly because of the colour of my skin. I'd felt uneasy about being olive-skinned when the National Front had set on us, but at the new school I was made to feel like I had the plague. I was too young and shy to deal with it, so I just withdrew more and more. In turn, the bullying only worsened. The problems with the National Front happened when I was in my home environment, and during those difficult times I'd always had my family around to physically protect me and guide me away from it. At school it was a totally different ballgame. I had no family to turn to and no one to show me how to protect myself.

I was afraid from my first day at St Mary's. The long grey pathway that led up to the school felt eerie and unwelcoming. As I walked up to the front door, I only wished that I could have stayed at home, alone and safe in my garden. I was right to be scared, for, when I met the other schoolgirls, they didn't welcome me at all.

I remember approaching a group of smartly dressed girls who were huddled together at the back of the classroom. They were busy flicking through a brightly coloured teen magazine and were giggling away at the pictures. I wanted to see what they were looking at and to join in. I was curious because I'd never been allowed to read a magazine like that, plus I was keen to make new friends.

'Can I sit with you?' I said timidly.

They looked up, snarled and ignored me.

'She smells,' said one of them.

'Look at her spots,' said another.

'She looks brown and horrible,' chimed a third. 'Yuk.'

And then they burst out laughing.

And so it went on for the next few weeks, months and years. Relentlessly, the girls at St Mary's mocked my skin colour and my spots. I was ugly, I would never have a boyfriend. I was a disgusting, greasy, ugly Paki.

At first, the comments made me feel dirty and ashamed to have different-coloured skin but, as the bullying worsened, I even began resenting my own culture. I feel terrible for having thought this, because I feel so different now, but, when I was victimised and bullied as a child, I hated being Asian.

I felt totally bombarded by aggression. It felt like it was

engulfing me 24/7. I'd known for a while that my parents had problems, but, once the screaming rows started in the kitchen, I knew their marriage was in dire straits.

Some mornings, while standing in the garden waiting for the train to pass, I'd hear my father shouting at my mother in the kitchen. I'd tremble on hearing his voice screeching over her. I would go back up to the house, stand at the kitchen door and watch in horror as they argued furiously.

At some point, Uncle Raja moved in with us. I was relieved because sometimes my uncle managed to intervene and break up the fights between my parents. But it turned out that the more my uncle intervened, the more my father became riled.

It became so common for my father to scold and hit my mother that after a while it became a part of our everyday lives. He would shout at my mother about silly things – perhaps she had too much salt in the curry or hadn't cleaned up properly that morning.

Even though Uncle Raja couldn't stop the arguments and disharmony, it was nice to finally see a happy friendly male face in the family. At first, my uncle was just that. He was a short, muscular man with longish hair and a long moustache. His big nose and funny laugh made him so endearing and, at ten years old, I loved spending time with him. 'You're so pretty, little Sofia,' he used to say, smiling down at me. 'Come and see me when you wake up tomorrow morning and brighten up my day.'

It felt great that someone had finally noticed me within our home, and I jumped at the chance to be showered with affection, love and attention at last. Uncle Raja's room was on the floor above us, so whenever I went to see him it was very private and secluded. Every morning after prayer time, I began skipping my time in the garden just to go upstairs and make him tea. 'Morning, Sofia,' he'd say from underneath the covers. 'Can you make me a cup of tea and then come over and sit with me?'

I felt comforted sitting on the edge of his bed. Even though we often sat in silence, just being there made me really happy. When he finished drinking his tea, we'd chat about the day ahead and what I was looking forward to doing at the weekend. I loved those mornings. I was finally bonding with someone, and I felt lucky that that someone was a man.

A few months later, we were having the usual cup of tea when my uncle said he wanted to kiss and hug me. I let him, although something didn't feel quite right. I didn't know any different at that age – I was used to aggression and I'd never been hugged or kissed by anyone, let alone my father and mother.

Over the months, Uncle Raja's hugs got longer and his kisses heavier. 'Can I kiss your lips, Sofia?' he'd ask, and before I knew it I'd feel his moustache brushing against my mouth. Soon, he started to say he wanted to touch my hair, my face and then other parts of my body. Again, it felt slightly wrong. I was nervous about his actions, but at that age I didn't know what he was doing, let alone what was right or wrong. All I remember feeling is that finally someone was caring for me.

My uncle was kind and always smiled at me when he touched me, so I didn't feel fear with him. Instead, I felt lucky that this warm, loving man had chosen me out of the family because he wanted *me* to make his tea and spend the morning with him. He wanted to hug and kiss *me*, not the others. 'I've finally got attention and love,' I used to say to myself when lonely at school or in bed at night. I had completely stopped going down to the train track within a few months of my uncle arriving at our home – his love and affection had finally filled the void. I felt important for the first time in my life and was valued by someone above my siblings. I finally had a friend and a father figure all in one person.

On some Saturday afternoons, my uncle took me for walks up the road. We'd walk hand in hand and he'd tell me exciting stories about Pakistan and other far-off countries. It was extremely interesting listening to his fascinating little stories and it always felt like I was escaping the dreary world that I lived in. My uncle knew full well how to feed my hunger for music and dance so he spent hours telling me wild stories about Bollywood stars and films that he'd seen. Sometimes, when he'd finished a particular story, we'd walk through a dark, desolate archway under a railway, where he'd kiss me and touch my body out of anyone's sight.

It was when we started spending time in the arch that I began to feel uncomfortable with him. Something was wrong. 'It's our little secret,' Uncle Raja would say softly as he stroked my hair. But because I wasn't at home I began to feel scared. I suppose my instinct kicked in and I started to feel more and more uncomfortable with what he was doing to me.

I became nervous around him and displayed a reluctance to be with him. I started to say 'no' when he asked me to go to the arch with him or even to make his tea. I'd begun to question the way my uncle was treating me and, of course, he started to notice a change.

'You've nothing to fear with me, Sofia,' he'd say, smiling

warmly. 'Tell me about your fears. You can trust me. You mustn't tell a soul about our little walks and morning-tea times, but you must still come and be with me. This is our little secret time and we're special to one another.' He said it over and over.

He bought me little presents to try to keep me happy and it worked for a while – I'd be over the moon when I unwrapped a box of chocolates or small toys. His gifts made me feel warm, loved and secure again, so I'd return to his bedroom each morning and sit on his bed before he kissed me.

Despite my growing fears and worries, the afternoon walks and morning teas went on for a year. Uncle Raja kept lavishing more sweets and gifts on me, but each time he offered me something, unfortunately, he started to expect more in return. He'd ask me to lie down next to him in his bed in the morning because he was cold, so I'd climb under the sheets. We'd lie close to one another in the bed and he'd stroke me.

One Saturday, my uncle asked me if I wanted to go on our usual walk. I was nearly 12 by then. He took me up the road to a clearing, then suddenly he pushed me to the ground behind some bushes. 'What are you doing, Uncle Raja?' I cried as he lunged on top of me. I was soon starting to suffocate as I struggled beneath him. It was so frightening and alien – I couldn't breathe as he started to kiss my mouth savagely. The feeling is still so clear in my mind. He held both of my arms down and my wrists were hurting from his grip. The bushes were scratching my skin and I felt pain where his erection was pushing on to my groin through his clothes. He was rocking his body up and down on top of me and as he did so he was pushing my legs open with his. He was breathing heavily and the sound was swamping my cries as I squirmed beneath him.

He unzipped his flies and pushed my skirt up and I knew that something really bad was about to happen. I went into survival mode, but the more I tried to break free the more he bore down on me with his body weight. Uncle Raja hadn't managed to penetrate me yet, and I knew I had to find the strength to escape before he did. God knows how, but I wriggled free. I managed to push him off me and, in that second, I got up off the floor and ran, pushing the bushes and brambles out of the way as I ran.

I ran all the way home and hid in the bedroom under my bunk bed. Uncle Raja didn't come home for a while, but I stayed safely under the bed just in case.

A few hours later, I heard him come in. 'Sofia, I've something for you. Are you upstairs?' I heard him call.

I froze and held my breath. I could feel my heart beating really fast and it sounded so loud to me that I hoped that he couldn't hear it. I heard his heavy footsteps on the treads, and he was soon crouching down and looking at me hiding from him under the bed. In his hands my uncle was clutching a pair of bright-red roller skates. A few days earlier, I'd told him about a particular pair of skates that I'd seen in Oxfam. They were the ones that you put your feet in and adjust the bottom to fit your foot. The base of each skate was silver and the foothold was bright-red leather. I'd always wanted roller skates like that, and I remember gasping when I saw them dangling there in front of my eyes.

After a few moments of staring, I looked at him and then back at the roller skates again. Out of fear, confusion and childlike need, I reached out and calmly accepted my uncle's bribe for my silence. I didn't say a word to him as I grabbed the skates and then ran as fast as I could outside.

I skated for hours that afternoon, coasting along the black tarmac path at the top of the garden. I ignored the pain in my body as I skated and I was glad that my trousers were covering the bloody scratches on my legs. I skated and skated and as the wheels hit the tarmac I tried hard to bury any thoughts of those awful moments by the bush with Uncle Raja.

The next morning, once Uncle Raja left the house for work, I knew that I needed to tell my mother. Through the night I'd felt so stupid and annoyed with myself for accepting the skates. In the end, I just wanted to give them back and for Uncle Raja to be punished. The only person who I thought I could go to was my mother. As I washed and dressed that morning, I hoped that she would tell Uncle Raja that he had to leave our home.

My mother was in the kitchen preparing the curry for the day, so I went downstairs, walked over to her by the cooker and took a deep breath. 'Uncle Raja asked me something rude yesterday, Mum, and he touched me somewhere rude,' I said softly. Instead of taking me in her arms, she just looked down at me blankly, and then a look of disappointment spread across her face. 'You shouldn't accept his gifts then, should you, Sofia,' she said curtly. 'Where are the skates he gave you? I saw you skating with them,' she asked, then turned her face back to the curry that was simmering on the hob.

I felt even worse now. I couldn't understand why my own mother wasn't going to help me. I remember running upstairs and wanting the comfort of my bed. I climbed in and lay shivering under the covers, thinking about what to do. I wanted protection but I had no idea where to get it, especially since the person who should have protected me had shunned me.

Funnily enough, my mother did come and see me an hour or so later. She came upstairs and looked down at me in bed. 'Are you going to be OK, Sofia?' she asked quietly.

'Sorry, please let me sleep,' I replied, and all she did was wander back downstairs.

Now I understand that my mother would have felt shame if she'd known the facts, and even more shame if anyone in the community ever found out about the decay and cancer that was growing in our family by the day. My mother wanted to believe that nothing untoward had happened within her supposedly upstanding, decent family. Believing that was so much safer for her. Still, in my youthful confusion, I felt helpless and guilty because she'd said it was my fault for taking the roller skates. I had no one to turn to that day and I felt more unloved than ever.

In the end, I also decided that my uncle's actions were better hushed up, but for my own reasons. I realised that, if I'd told her exactly what my uncle had done and my father had found out, then I'd come to harm at my dad's hands. I knew full well that my father would beat me. On pain of death, I felt I had to keep it a secret. Sadly, the pain that I'd suffered that evening was only the beginning.

Later that night, my mother came back into our bedroom again. 'Think about what you say to me in future,' she began. 'No one in the family would hurt you and you know it. You're a liar if you say that someone in the family has harmed you. If you spread lies outside the family, it'll only get you into more trouble. It will bring you harm.'

And then she left the room. She was right about the harm, but it still hurt so deeply that my mother had put the family honour before her own daughter's health and safety. As the hours ticked by, I sank deeper into depression because the pain just wouldn't go away. By midnight I was at rock bottom. I got out of bed and went into the bathroom. I took a packet of paracetemol from the cupboard and swallowed the pills, one by one. I know that I needed to feel physical pain as well as emotional pain. Inside, I'd never felt a deeper more emotional pain than this so I didn't know what else to do.

I went back to bed, but instead of falling asleep and numbing the pain, I suddenly started to panic. 'Mum, Mum,' I cried out. Everyone else was asleep in the bedroom but she heard me whimpering in the darkness. 'Help me,' I said as she rushed towards my bed.

'What have you done now, Sofia?' she asked concerned. 'Are you pregnant?'

I couldn't believe what she was saying.

'You said I was a liar but Uncle Raja hurt me,' I sobbed. 'I've taken some pills because I want to die. No one loves me here and everyone is hurting me.'

The bedroom was so dark that I couldn't see my mother's face, but I noticed that her breathing stopped for a second. She then rushed downstairs and came back with a pint of milk. 'Drink this, Sofia, and it'll make you feel better.' That was all she said; then she climbed back into her bed. There was no hug, no warm word, no 'I love you'.

I felt terrible. I was sick that night as I kept on drinking the milk. I just remember feeling numb the next day.

From that day, I knew that I no longer wanted to be a part of a family that was riddled with aggression, restriction and deceit. I knew that one day I might have to leave my family.

Looking back, my first contact and relationships with men were terrible. I only knew violence and aggression from my father, and then the affection that I had from my uncle was so warped and wrong. As a child, I never knew what real love and affection was and that impacted on me greatly as I progressed through my teenage years and into my twenties.

CHAPTER FIVE

DRAWING BLOOD

Self-harming is an extreme form of need. Yet the reason I self-harmed was clear enough. I'd already started to cut myself when my father had become angry with me in the shop for eating chocolate, but they were never deep cuts. They were small, surface scratches that I'd etch out on my arm with a pin or needle when I was alone, locked away in the bathroom. Whenever my father punished me or I'd had a bad day with the bullies at school, I'd often find my mother's sewing kit, get a pin and run up there with it and shut the door. I'd sit on the loo, scratch my arm and watch the thin lines of blood seep through the skin on my wrists. Those scratches weren't too painful, but they gave me a small, comforting release from the other pain in my life. Hurting myself gave me comfort, and that's all that mattered back then.

When I was finished, I would run the sink full of water and wash the blood away. I would watch the water disappear down the plughole and feel much better.

Sometimes I'd also do things like staple myself in my leg or wet my hands and stick them over the plug sockets hoping that I'd get electrocuted. But, as life got worse, my self-harming became more extreme.

My next school was Chapter High School in nearby Strood. There, the bullying only worsened. The girls used to pick fights with me on a regular basis and sometimes we'd end up getting into catty scrambles outside the school gates.

There were two main bullies, I'll call them Christine and Jackie, who seemed to hate me with a passion. They gave me at least two black eyes during my time there. Again the bullying was centred on my nose, spots and skin colour. The difference was that because we were older – I was 13 – the bullying had become much more violent. The girls would often want to fight me when it was home time and they never worried about how hard, or even where, they hit me.

The more I was bullied, the more I wanted to throw myself into music and acting. I realised that these two positive things in my life made me feel happy and safe. I joined the recorder club and had acted in almost all of the school plays, and I knew that these creative things had a positive impact on me. Whenever I was immersed in acting or singing, just like when I daydreamed at home or in the garden, my mind escaped the problems I'd been having. It's strange to think that, despite feeling lonely and afraid everywhere and anywhere I was, I could always get up on stage and dance or sing in front of everyone without a care in the world. It just shows how passionate I was about it all.

I remember hearing the other school kids chat about an amazing new pop star called Michael Jackson. Sometimes they brought his cassettes into school and played them during our lunch breaks. I'd sit alone at the back of the classroom and feel captivated by the sound of Michael's fantastic voice. Without looking up, I'd copy down the lyrics and then watch the girls get up and act out Michael's dance moves. At home I wasn't allowed to listen to such music because of my father's tight rules, so whatever pop music I heard during these times at school was always kept secret from him in case he punished me.

My parents became aware of my increasing interest in dance and music, but they hoped it was just a phase. They allowed me to join the recorder club and do any plays I wanted, but things changed dramatically when I entered a talent show. I had decided to copy the Michael Jackson moves that I'd seen the other girls do, and for months I practised tirelessly for the show. I'd written down the lyrics for 'The Way You Make Me Feel' and had learned the moves by heart from secretly watching the video.

I wasn't even nervous on the day of the show. When the curtain went up, I stood there in my school uniform and felt nothing but a buzz of excitement when the music started. I saw a sea of expectant faces in front of me and in my heart all I wanted to do was make them happy. I wanted everyone in front of me to thoroughly enjoy my performance. But, when I started to dance, I spotted my friends looking and laughing at me – one of the moves was obviously sexual and at that age and in my innocence I had no idea. That was what they found so funny.

Little did I know that within a week gossip about my 'crude' dance had engulfed the whole Asian community. Naturally, my parents were very upset. 'You looked like a cheap woman, Sofia. Everyone is saying it,' my father screamed at me in the living room. 'Who's this Michael

Jackson man and do you know what those moves you were doing actually looked like?' he shouted, grabbing my shoulders and shaking me hard.

I had humiliated the family, he told me. I had been doing dirty things on stage for everyone to see. Other parents would be ashamed. I had tarnished our honour. 'You aren't allowed to perform again,' he said. Then he shoved me up the stairs to my room, and told me to stay there. 'Music and acting is a form of prostitution, Sofia,' he shrieked up after me.

I lay face down on my pillow and the tears flowed. I felt angry and wanted to fight back. I loved dancing and singing so much. But I knew that my life depended on obeying him.

When I finally hit puberty, my father clamped down on me harder than he had done over the music. He began seeing changes and they were changes that weren't what he wanted to see in his daughter. We all had various duties to do at home and the females were given a much stricter regime as they grew up. I had to take it in turns with my sisters to do things for my father like shirt ironing and shoe polishing, and making his chutney. I knew that if I didn't give his things to him in mint condition then I'd be punished.

One Sunday afternoon, I'd been allowed to play in the field opposite my house. I knew that I needed to be careful to keep within my parents' view. When one of the male neighbours walked past the field and waved at me, I waved back. My father saw and punished me. He shot out of the house and dragged me back inside, shouting at me all the time.

At that point, I could obey my father's rule of not allowing me to interact with boys, because I wasn't especially interested in them. The issue of enjoying my femininity was a much more difficult and pressing one for me. I desperately wanted to start to enjoy my femininity like the other girls at school. I'd already had my music taken away from me but I'd always felt that my femininity was a natural gift and part of me that needed to flourish. I started to experiment with clothes and make-up like everyone else, but stupidly I didn't think of the consequences.

I must have been about 13 when I went into Boots in Gravesend to try on a lipstick for the first time. I was out of my father's view and so got stuck in. 'Look at my pink lips!' I remember squealing to my sisters as I pouted in the mirror at the make-up counter. I remember loving the colour that the lipstick injected into my sallow olive skin, and I felt pretty and feminine for the first time ever.

'You need to clean it off before we get home,' my sister Saira warned me, handing me a tissue. 'Dad will really scold you if he sees that on your face.'

Fearing the worst, I obeyed and wiped the beautiful colour from my lips. I felt sad as we walked home because I knew that wearing make-up might actually make me prettier and perhaps enable me to fit in with the other girls at school.

I'd left a smudge stain on my bottom lip, thinking that my father wouldn't even notice it. But he spotted it straight away and told me to stay in the bathroom until it was washed off. 'Don't come out until you've scrubbed yourself clean,' he said. 'Make-up is banned in our house. You know the rules and yet seem to constantly disobey them.'

I stayed in the bathroom until darkness fell. I sat and looked at my face in the mirror for hours because I wanted my moment of enjoyment to last just a while longer. After two or three hours, I filled the bathroom sink with hot water, washed my face clean and went back downstairs.

My worst scolding happened the afternoon we all went to the amusement park at Margate. Unknowingly, I'd wandered off further than I'd thought – I always found myself wandering off at home or on family outings without even knowing that I was doing it. Deep down, I always wanted to escape the restrictions I felt trapped by, so perhaps my wandering off was an unconscious way of attempting to. Regardless, I never got very far.

When we got to Margate, Dad told us where the meeting point was, and what time we had to be back. 'If you want to go off, then everyone needs to be back under this tree in an hour.' he said.

It was midday. I wandered off and got back half an hour later because I wanted to have a ride on a rollercoaster and then got sidetracked by a bunch of children on the way back. They were happily playing and dancing to the music around the Punch and Judy stall. I watched, smiling at them and wanting to join in. I noticed how free, happy and easy they were, and I quickly lost track of time.

My father was seething when I eventually turned up. Everyone else was waiting with him under the tree. As soon as he saw me, he lost his temper and began to shout at me. He shouted so loudly and went on for so long that eventually a crowd started to gather, desperate to see what the commotion was. It was so embarrassing.

We all became so petrified of my father, but we

eventually accepted his behaviour as a way of life. That said, the trauma it caused me then, and later on, ran deep.

The first time that I self-harmed with a blade was on a day when we had visitors at our house. They'd brought along a newborn baby. I suddenly felt warm and protected as I held the baby in our living room. It was as if he was mine to love unconditionally. He was a tiny, three-month-old boy called Humza.

Humza was so gorgeous. I remember him babbling and smiling up at me as I looked into his tiny, brown, button-like eyes. He looked so innocent and it felt beautiful cradling him in my arms. I was overwhelmed with a real and natural love – something I'd never experienced within my own home. My cousins were there too, and we fussed and cooed over pretty little Humza. I was in a bubble of happiness, but all too soon one of my sisters took him out of my arms.

'What are you doing? Let me hold him a few minutes longer,' I pleaded. But it was too late; they had already given him back to his mother.

'That's enough, Sofia. You've had enough time with him today. Go and clean up the bedroom,' said my sister, Tahira.

I took it badly – I loved Humza and had felt as if he had loved me back and now he was being taken away from me. Once again, I felt alone and bullied, so I ran up to the bathroom and looked at myself sobbing in the mirror.

I found my father's razor blade in the cabinet above the sink and quickly slashed my arms. I sat on the floor in floods of tears as the pain seared through my arms and blood began to cover the floor. I remember thinking that, if they saw my damaged arm, and the blood, then they'd surely come and hug me and even give the baby back. I somehow felt they were punishing me when they took Humza out of my arms because they'd taken away my precious moment of love and happiness.

I stayed upstairs in the bathroom and eventually started to howl. I was so weak that I couldn't get up. Although I was scared by how weak I was, I wanted to see the harm through; I wanted someone to find me in this shocking state, so that perhaps they would feel sorry for me and hug me.

I heard my cousin knock at the door. 'Are you OK, Sofia?' she whispered.

'No, I'm bleeding. Go away,' I said, weak and confused.

But she pushed open the door and gasped when she saw all the blood. She cried out and ran downstairs to get help.

I could hear everybody whispering among themselves for a while, and then my mother came upstairs and bandaged my arms up quickly.

'You need to stop doing this,' she said. 'You're not to do this any more.'

'They took the baby away,' I said, forlorn. 'It's not fair. Why can't I ever have any love?'

In response, my mum went to fetch the baby from my sisters, hoping it would calm me down.

My mother never addressed the issue afterwards. It was such an extreme thing for a child to have done, but all my mother did was bandage my arm up, clean the floor and take me back downstairs. She never asked me about the cuts, or how I felt inside or if she could do anything to help me. As far as she was concerned, the issue was completely dead and buried after that. It had been just the same with the Uncle Raja incident. Once again, it was the issue of family honour that took precedence over everything else. It was easier for my mother to pretend none of it had ever happened.

Self-harming is a short-term comfort, and at 18 I finally stopped doing it. When I got to university and was away from home, the need for me to relieve my pain lessened. I'm glad that I didn't die because I have so much to live for, so much to do with my life. If someone had spoken to me when I was self-harming and told me that my life would change and that I was worthy of being loved, I think it might have helped me. I felt at the time as though I had no one to turn to and was worth nothing. I was basing how I felt on what others thought of me – but now I know that the only opinion about me that matters is my own. I will not let anyone make me feel bad about who I am – no one has the right to make you feel bad, make you cry or feel worthless. We all have the right to be happy and loved. For other girls out there who self-harm I'd say, 'Look forward to a time when you grow and can find yourself because your life is a gift and you are a special person.'

I have scars from the self-harming, and I still don't know what I'll tell my children when they ask about them. I'll cross that bridge when I come to it.

On the subject of bullying, there is a light at the end of the tunnel but I think that it only appears once we are physically removed from it. We can't remove ourselves as children but, in an adult environment, we do have more of a choice. More often than not, we can walk away from it. As children, we are placed in schools where we cannot just walk away from a bully. Those being bullied should tell a teacher, a parent or a close friend – someone will be able to help you. There are also professionals you can talk to – I used to call ChildLine. I didn't know who they were but at least I had someone to talk to.

CHAPTER SIX

TEENAGE MARRIAGE

It must have been the Michael Jackson incident that triggered my parents' initial desire to find me a husband. The dance was too sexual for them, and the Asian community in general, so, before I got any other ideas about boyfriends and such things, they thought it best to find me a husband. But when I began self-harming and attempting to show off my femininity, they began looking into it formally. Mum and Dad were extremely concerned about my breaking the family honour. Little did I know that marrying me off, or shipping me off to Pakistan, was, in their opinion, the only option.

I've never met a woman who has wanted, let alone been happy in, an arranged marriage. People often tell me they can work, but I've yet to see a successful one. The process of arranging a marriage involves a meeting where a boy and a girl are introduced. If they get on, the parents quickly arrange the marriage for a time when everyone is ready.

Most girls don't get a choice in the matter and this can breed deep unhappiness – with a family's honour in mind, divorce is not really an option. If divorce crops up then shame, punishment and, in some cases, death can be the outcome for the woman in the relationship.

I was nearly 14 when my mother whisked me off to Pakistan to meet my potential husband, although I was completely unaware of her intentions.

'I'm taking you to meet your family in Pakistan, Sofia,' she had said over breakfast one morning. 'It'll do you some good.'

I was amazed, and wondered why it was only me that was going with her. Still, I was curious and excited about the adventure.

'We're flying next week,' said Mum. 'I want you to get to know our family over there.'

I didn't question my mother's motives, I just relished the chance to meet my Pakistani family, to find out if our culture was the same in Pakistan, and to see if I might fit in better there.

I was so excited as we packed our suitcases that weekend. 'I'm so looking forward to going on a plane!' I said, imagining myself flying through the sky like a bird. I'd never flown before or even seen the inside of an airport.

On the morning of our flight, I remember wandering down the garden to wait for the train one final time. As it went by, I waved at the passengers happily – in my mind I was going to a much more exciting place than they could ever imagine. I felt so lucky. For once I felt more special than my siblings – they were staying home under the watchful eye of my father, while I was jetting off to an amazing, far-off land.

We were poor, so we couldn't take a direct flight to Islamabad. I sat quietly next to my mother on the flight and watched all the passengers and crew milling about around us. 'You can't leave your seat unless you need the toilet, Sofia. You must try and get some sleep,' she said.

But I couldn't sleep and sat with my face pressed against the tiny window. I was intrigued by the sky and by what lay ahead in my homeland, Pakistan. Some passengers prayed in the aisles once the flight was under way and I remember thinking how devout they were.

My mother's sister and her kids picked us up outside Islamabad airport and, although I was exhausted, I couldn't close my eyes as we drove through the sprawling, dusty city. There was so much to take in that I was mesmerised. There were open sewers by the roadsides so the roads were very smelly and black. Women and children sat begging or watching the time go by at the roadsides. My mother had given me some spare money at the airport, so when we stopped off to get some water I got out of the car and began handing it out to the kids and women who flocked around me. I felt guilty that I had nice clothes on and a clean face when they were dirty and dressed in rags. It was strange, for in England we were poor, but in Pakistan I felt really rich and therefore wanted to share what I had. After a few minutes, my mother stopped me handing out my money, and said it was too dangerous, so I got back into the car and tried to sleep.

The outskirts of the city were much nicer. We drove to Abbottobad, a village in the rolling green mountains. I spotted buffalo wallowing in aqua-blue rivers to cool off from dry heat, and girls filling their clay pots with water from the fresh streams before carrying them on their heads along the dusty roads. They were strikingly pretty and the air was clean. I'd been struck by the sheer poverty and dirt in the bustling city that lay behind me. Now I was struck by the beauty of the countryside. The road through the mountains was bumpy and uncomfortable in the rickety old car, but I didn't care because I felt so in love with it all. As I finally drifted off to sleep, I thought of my bunk bed back in Gravesend and of wandering about in the garden. I felt as if I'd been transported into another world.

After about an hour, I woke up when we stopped to find a toilet. I had to squat over a tiny muddy hole in the ground while my mother held on to me tightly so that I didn't fall in.

'We need to be careful and wash our hands, Sofia – we might fall ill if we don't. Our bodies aren't used to the water here,' my mother told me.

It's normal to fall ill over there if you've been accustomed to standards of hygiene in the western world. In spite of my mother's caution, I did go down with a stomach bug. It was painful and a shock to my system, but at that age you always seem to recover more quickly from illnesses like that.

After several hours, we finally arrived at my grandfather's house. The house was made of grey stone and lay at the foot of some very beautiful hills that towered into the blue sky. His wasn't a bad house, considering the poverty around us. It seemed Grandfather was a lot better off than most people there.

I stepped out of the car, stretched my aching limbs and looked around, savouring the beauty around. Funnily, I remember imagining I was a princess in a Bollywood movie!

'You must be Sofia,' said a voice.

I turned and saw a friendly-looking old man, then realised I must be looking at my grandfather! I felt a rush of warmth come over me and ran into his arms. We hugged one another tightly. I'd never met him before, so it was really nice to see this magical old man smiling at me, full of love. He reminded me of the wizard Merlin.

'Where can I play, Grandfather?' I said.

'There'll be plenty of time for that later on,' he said, smiling warmly and ushering us into the house. 'Now you run inside and get undressed for your bath. You must be tired and hungry after the long trip.'

He showed us our big room, which had concrete walls and no carpet. There wasn't a proper bathroom in the house, so we wandered down the garden with towels on into a concrete room. We filled a big steel bath with hot water and I climbed in. My mother poured water over me using a small plastic bucket. It found it difficult to get used to at first, but soon I was enjoying myself – it was part of my new adventure, after all.

I really loved spending time with my grandfather. He was so warm and kind to me. In the mornings we got up to pray before the sun rose. You could hear the *azaan* call to prayer five times a day, and I loved it. I felt like I was living in a mystical, fairytale world. Every day, fresh icy water from the mountains would be piped to the house, and there was so much exploring to do. Grandfather allowed me to wander off when I wanted to and best of all he constantly remarked how pretty I was. During those first few days, I felt protected, happy and loved. No one was bullying me and my father was a million miles away. I felt free and loved by my grandfather and for once it felt like my mother was there if I needed her. She seemed happier and calmer too, and we even started to laugh and play together. It was the way things ought to be between a mother and daughter.

My grandfather bought me a doll called Helen. I loved her because she spoke when you pushed her belly button. She had big blue eyes, pale skin and blonde hair.

'She's pretty just like you are, Sofia,' Grandfather said as he watched me brush her long blonde hair with one of his combs.

I felt so happy when he said that because my doll was pretty, and of course I wanted to look like her.

The next week, my mother suddenly told me that we had to travel to another place where I was to meet a little boy. 'You can spend the day playing together, Sofia. He's your cousin Pomi and he can't wait to meet you,' she said, smiling warmly at me. 'If you like each other, you can play together forever.'

I don't remember feeling worried, or suspecting that she was introducing me to my future husband, but looking back I remember that I just wanted to stay in Pakistan with my grandfather, my mother and Helen.

It was on this trip that I remember seeing happiness in my mother for the first time. When she told me about Pomi, she actually reached out and hugged me – I felt like I'd finally won her affection and wanted to please her more than ever. I remember thinking, If meeting Pomi would make her happy then I'll be happy too. I really felt content when we left my grandfather's house that morning. Finally, I thought, I might have a friend.

My aunty (Dad's sister) lived in the mountains on the northwest border with China and Afghanistan. I couldn't wait to get there to meet my new friend and cousin. 'You'll like him. He's really sweet natured,' explained Mum in the car. 'When we arrive I'm going to spend time with your aunty and you two can play.'

When I met my prospective husband, I thought he was so cute. I really did like Pomi. He was tall, lean, smiley and very nice. We played with his toys on the balcony and Pomi gave me tons of attention, which felt good. Pomi even agreed to come and visit me at my grandfather's house so I could show him my doll Helen. We got on so well that when my mother finally came on to the balcony with my aunt I asked if we could stay longer.

'You can see Pomi again, Sofia,' said Mum. 'If you like him you can marry him.' I remember feeling really happy inside when she blurted that out. Not only would I have a friend, but I'd also have a proper boyfriend! At that moment thoughts of an arranged marriage still hadn't entered my mind – I was bowled over by Pomi and, being a romantic girl, I thought it was love at first sight. I felt we were destined to be together.

I'd heard about arranged marriages, of course. Although they'd worried me before, standing with Pomi on the balcony in the beautiful mountains of Pakistan made it all feel so right. In my mind, even if mine and Pomi's would be an arranged marriage, it didn't matter. My mind raced as I imagined having a *Nika*, which is like an engagement, and then I thought how at 18 I'd have an official marriage ceremony.

'Yes, I will marry him, Mum!' I smiled, thinking of what the bullies at school had told me. 'Pomi is a nice boy,' I added gleefully. I was so happy, and desperate to fly back home and tell the schoolgirls that they were so wrong. I *was* going to have a boyfriend after all.

Looking at him, I thought that Pomi was my knight in shining armour. Meeting him was so amazing that I even forgot about my singing and acting dreams. I thought it was all settled and organised. I told my mum how happy I was that she'd brought me here, and how much I liked Pomi.

Then, suddenly, everything fell apart.

When I went to the bathroom, I overheard my aunt talking to my mother. 'She isn't what he wants, Surriya,' said my aunt. 'Pomi doesn't think she's pretty enough. I'm so sorry. What about Saira? Can you bring her?'

My heart sank as I stared at my face in the mirror. I looked at my spotty skin and my big nose and I thought I understood why I wasn't good enough. I wasn't pretty at all. The schoolgirls had been right all along. Then my eyes filled with tears as I imagined that my grandfather had just been lying about how pretty I was, just as Pomi had. I knew that he'd much prefer my pretty little sister Saira.

I looked around the bathroom and my eyes settled on a pair of sharp nail scissors by the big steel bathtub. I picked them up and quickly made a small cut about two inches up my right wrist and let the blood bubble up over my skin. There wasn't much blood because the cut wasn't deep enough, but it certainly eased the pain. Then I washed my hands and wrists, cleaned my face and tidied up my hair. I felt better when I went downstairs.

After the comfort from the cut had subsided, all I could think about was my doll, Helen. I wanted to be with her and hug her and then take her straight home to Britain. I wanted to get back to my garden and climb underneath my bed where I could write on my writing pad. I wanted to be where no one could hurt, reject or upset me any longer.

When I left Pomi's house that afternoon I was polite, and didn't show him that I was hurt. I shook his hand as, in my culture, hugging him would seem forward and make me look cheap. He just looked away. 'Bye, Sofia,' he murmured. 'You take care.'

We drove straight back to my grandfather's in silence. From that day onwards, my mother became distant again. She probably thought that I'd failed her.

When my mother and I arrived back at Northcote Road and got into our bunk beds, my mother told me a half-truth. 'Pomi's parents wanted someone younger, so you can't marry him,' she said. 'We do need to find you a husband, though. It's the only way you'll be able to enjoy a better and much more decent life.'

She switched the light off in our bedroom. I lay there, clutching Helen in the dark. I no longer cared about Pomi or them finding me a husband. I'd been rejected enough and I just wanted to be alone.

My younger sister Saira married Pomi and they had a child together. They ended up getting a divorce shortly after, and years later Pomi contacted me on the Internet. I started getting anonymous emails from someone who seemed to know a lot about me. One day the email said I was sexy and had grown up to be beautiful. I wanted to know who all these compliments were coming from, so wrote back and asked.

'It's me, Pomi,' read the reply.

I deleted the message straight away.

CHAPTER SEVEN

FACTORY GIRL

'I want to see you working hard, Sofia,' my father said on my 14th birthday. 'Zarqa already earns a decent wage at the apple-packing factory. Now you can go to work so that you can afford to buy your own things. It'll keep you out of mischief and involve you in something decent for a change.' I was to go the recruitment agency after school the next day.

All the women in our family became factory girls at some point during our childhood. Once we were old enough, it became as integral to our lives as praying and fasting. The work was hard and the hours were long, but spending the weekends in a factory suited me fine because it meant that I was out of the house and finally able to earn some money of my own.

Having some pocket money would be a real bonus. I'd started wanting to buy things like a Walkman and a new pair of school shoes and I obviously couldn't ever ask my parents for those things, so, just as Zarqa had done a few years before, the day after my 14th birthday I rang the employment agency in Gravesend and told them that I wanted to come in and see them. The next day I went in for the interview, and the next weekend was my first working day.

I got up at 4am because Zarqa and I had to make enough time to fit in our prayers, chores and breakfast before we left for work at 5am. We had to meet the other factory workers in Gravesend and then sit on a bus for two hours, heading for the countryside.

Although I was tired, when the sun came up, I felt excited about my day ahead. I remember looking round the bus at all the other Asian, Eastern European and British faces. They all looked so pale, drawn and tired. Some were still sleeping with their caps pulled over their eyes, and others were just staring blankly out of the bus window. I wasn't worried though – I noticed straight away that they were all much older than Zarqa and I were.

This is my first day at work! I thought, smiling. 'I'm in the big wide world!' I said to my sister.

'Hush now, Sofia,' she replied.

When the bus stopped, Zarqa ushered me off it and into the factory as quickly as she could. It was so noisy inside. There were forklift trucks ploughing through the middle of the huge room, and each one carried fifty or so boxes at a time, all overflowing with yellow, green and red apples.

When I spotted the manager's office, I knocked on the door, went in and introduced myself. He was small and had a friendly face and thick brown hair. He smiled, gave me a blue and white overall and hat, and told me to work near my sister

I stood next to Zarqa by the conveyor belt and watched

her pick out any bad apples that she spotted on the thick black belt. I did as I was told and stood there for hours and hours watching hundreds of apples pass by while Zarqa told me which ones she was binning. I noticed there were huge overflowing bins of rotten apples at the back of the factory. All I could hear was the buzzing and whirring of the machines and the conveyor belt, and the manager shouting at his staff. It was difficult to hear what Zarqa was saying at times, but after a while I got used to it.

Despite the smell and noise, it felt good working and I did the best I could there. After a while I was so adept at sorting through the apples that I was moved to the apple-packing section, which was fortunately a bit quieter. Some of the adults became friends who would give me sweets and biscuits and make a fuss of me because I was young, and I soon grew to love the whole factory experience. I enjoyed being away from my house every weekend, and being given responsibility. I started to come out of my shell in that factory because it took me away from the misery of life at home and allowed me to interact with different people.

Earning money was the best thing ever. The wages were low, but I could earn up to £50 a week if I did both days at the weekend and even more when I worked longer hours. I'd get home on the Sunday night and always buy my mother a gift from my wages. My father didn't treat her at all, so I wanted to make her happy and bought her things like flowers, clothes or a nice pair of slippers. The rest was for me to spend in the week.

I'll never forget my first pay packet. I took a deep breath and slowly counted out ten crisp twenty-pound notes. I'd never seen so much money at once, let alone felt it resting in my own palm. The first thing I bought was a nice cassette Walkman. It cost ten pounds and I'd seen it in Woolworth's months beforehand. I was so excited when I got it because I could listen to what I wanted to, when I wanted to. And because I'd earned the money myself my father never complained.

Unfortunately, the apple-factory work dried up after six months. The agency found us other shift work at a nearby industrial laundry. My other sister Saira joined Zarqa and I, and it was nice having both of them with me on the bus journey. But when we got there for the 6am shift we soon realised that the conditions in the new factory were really terrible.

It was really hot and sticky and there was so much steam everywhere that I couldn't see more than two feet in front of me. The machines were loud and dangerous and we all had to shout when we spoke to anyone. It was truly awful, and I felt bad for Saira because I knew she'd really hate working in there. Also because she'd never worked before I assumed it would be a huge shock to her system. The laundry that we were doing came from hospitals and hotels. Saira often found soiled pants from patients in hospitals who had hidden them in the bedding. It was vile!

'Let's just get on with our work and chat about things together over lunch,' I said when we'd taken our places by a huge washing vat.

Our job involved stopping and starting the machines when the other older and more experienced workers told us to, and putting the soiled garments and sheets through a cleaning machine. Saira had her machine, Zarqa hers and I had mine. It was simple enough, but as the hours ticked by the factory became hotter and hotter and we often felt faint through heat and lack of drinking water. After the washing machines had finished, we were moved over to the dryers and that section was even hotter. The worst part of the day was working at the big pressing machine. It was massive, and we had to take hold of a sheet with someone else and lay it between two rollers. The machine would grab it and then all this steam came out as it ironed and dried the sheet. It was a dangerous machine – I remember feeling scared because there was a man working with it who had only four fingers. He told us the next day that he'd lost one in the machine, so after that we were all even more careful.

We only got one half-hour break during those day shifts. To signal it, a bell would sound and the machines would stop automatically. We'd troop into a small concrete room lit by a single light bulb and eat our packed lunches in silence because our ears would be hurting from the noisy machines and our mouths would be dry from dehydration. We drank as much as we could in that half-hour break. Then we'd return to our machines till 5pm.

Every night when we got home I'd climb straight into bed and fall fast asleep, but I'd often wake up a few hours later because my mouth was still parched and there was a horrible buzzing sound in my ears.

To make things even worse, I started being bullied at work. It was purely racial abuse and it always happened after work on the bus journey back home. I'd get called 'Paki' and 'big nose' and once again was told that I had horrible spots. I couldn't understand why it was happening again, but it was, and only to me. My sisters didn't seem to attract the bullies, and, if they did, they hid it from me. I do remember them being quiet and reserved compared to the other workers, though. I felt ugly, and whenever I climbed on to the bus I'd keep my head down and stay quiet. I wanted to make sure that no one had any reason to talk to or notice me.

My sisters knew what was happening but we knew that they could never stand up for me for fear of getting bullied themselves, and there was no way I was going to let that happen. I told them to remain quiet and that I'd deal with it. The only thing I could do was find a seat on my own near the driver, where I felt slightly safer.

Just when I was getting myself back on track, my confidence really started to founder again. As a result, I started to self-harm heavily. It was easy to get away with it because I could blame any new scars that appeared on my arms and legs on the heavy machinery. The self-harming was all I could do to numb the pain. I was spiralling into misery again.

Then, out of the blue, one of the recruitment-agency managers took a shine to me and offered me some protection. I'll call him Richard. All was not lost, it seemed.

Richard had a nice warm face and big blue eyes and I felt that I could trust him. He was 45 years old and a bit chubby, but very friendly. He'd obviously noticed that I'd started to sit alone during the workers' lunch break and on the bus, and whenever he walked up and down the room doing his daily headcount he stopped and smiled down at me reassuringly.

As I stood waiting at the back of the queue to get on the bus home one Saturday, Richard came over and offered me a lift home. 'You don't need to get on the bus with the others,' he said. 'I just want to make sure everything is OK for you.'

That Saturday, and every one after that, Richard gave

me a lift home. We always did it secretly so that the other workers wouldn't notice. I'd wander round to the car park at the back of the factory where Richard would be waiting in his car. I felt comfortable with Richard. He never asked me any questions, and it was so nice not dreading the journey home with the other girls. At least I could avoid the bullies this way.

Once we got near my house, I'd thank Richard for the lift and wait with him until my two sisters walked up the road to find me – I never wanted my father to see me in a strange man's car, so we remained out of sight until they showed up.

One night, Richard leaned over and tried to kiss me. I was shocked because I thought we were friends and that he was protecting me from harm. But that kiss suddenly changed everything. Richard was my employer and was supposed to be looking out for me, and nothing else. I felt so let down, but was determined not to let anyone take advantage of me this time. After all I'd been through at home and at school, I had to find the strength to stand up for myself. I sat in the car for a few more minutes, then acted.

I got out of his car, slammed the door behind me and walked back home with my head held high.

I didn't cry when I got home. I didn't self-harm. I didn't need to do either because I had decided to take control of the situation.

As I lay in bed that night, I decided I had to find another job. It was a simple decision. As soon as I'd made my decision, I drifted off to sleep.

Richard's behaviour had triggered something in me. Back in his car I'd realised that I could find exit points from the vicious circle of bullying, violation, abuse and restriction at home and at school. I thought that if I took small steps to control myself and my life, and also tried to move on from my past, then things might begin to improve for me.

CHAPTER EIGHT
FLIGHT TO FREEDOM

Just as I was about to turn 16, I landed a weekend job at the local Tesco. Tesco seemed a good choice as it was within walking distance of our house and the wages there were much better. Anyway, I started working at the checkouts and later on progressed to stock control. The job was quite fun, and the other women who worked there were really kind and friendly towards me, which was so nice.

As I'd done with my weekend job, I decided to take control of my school situation too. I researched all the local schools and found a mixed one called The Hundred Of Hoo School, which was also in Gravesend. I'd heard it was relaxed, had excellent standards and was fun. I was worried Mum and Dad would not let me move schools, but I told them the academic standards were better and they agreed to let me sign up and attend.

It was a good move. At my new school I felt I was making a brand-new start, and I loved it as anticipated.

Things also improved at home because my parents saw me working hard at Tesco at the weekends and doing well at school. Everyone seemed happier around me and I felt I was making good progress at putting my past behind me. Instead of being scared, I started pushing myself to be friendly towards other kids, and to my delight I was soon a popular member of the year. Gone was the bullied, ugly chick from Chapter High School. I'd set my heart on trying to become an invigorating new girl with heaps of love to give, and was finally being accepted.

During my final year at school, I thought long and hard about my future. I was almost 18 years old and, deep down, I still wanted to leave home and perhaps even perform, so I applied to Sussex University. My parents were in two minds about allowing me to go because I'd be away from home, but at the same time they wanted me to further my education and get a decent job. I think they were swayed to let me go because I'd decided to take Biology and Management – I knew full well that doing that course would please them!

Before the first term of university started, I found a room in a pretty street in Regency Square, near Brighton seafront. I was to share a bathroom and kitchen with other students, but it was clean and quiet and safe. When my mother took me to view the room, I overheard her having a quiet word with the landlord when I was upstairs in the bathroom.

'We'll take the room, Mr Hewson, but you're responsible for my daughter's honour now,' she said. 'She isn't allowed out after 9pm and she isn't to have men in her bedroom. If you notice any trouble, then you will need to telephone me immediately.'

The landlord probably didn't fully understand what my mother meant by 'honour', but I think he knew what she was really getting at, which was no boys and no nights out.

The next week I happily packed my bags and asked my parents to drive me down to Brighton. 'I've already spoken to your landlord, Sofia,' said Mum in the car. 'He's agreed to carry on maintaining our family rules, so please respect him and what I've asked him to do. If you start to disobey, we'll be driving you straight home.'

'Yes, Mum,' I said.

Mum's rule-laying came as no surprise. I accepted it as always and simply looked forward to my course and finally enjoying some time away from home.

When we arrived in Brighton, I skipped up the stairs to my new bedroom and waited for my father to unload the car. I felt so happy that day and all I wanted was for my parents to be happy for me too. I was doing everything in the way that they wanted and I was pleased that things had come this far. I could hear my mother chatting to the landlord again downstairs, but instead of her thrashing out her rules again I heard her laughing, so felt relieved that everything was going so smoothly. Despite my yearning to be independent and to leave home, I still wanted them to feel satisfied with the move and unstressed about it, as I guessed dealing with their first child leaving home would still be tough for them.

Unfortunately the situation soon deteriorated quite rapidly.

'Hi. I'm Max,' said the smiling young man who appeared in the hallway. 'I'm here with my girlfriend, and I live in the next room. If you ever need anything please don't hesitate to ask.'

'Thanks,' I shouted after him as he went into his room.

I looked out of the bedroom window and saw that my father was still lifting my bags and boxes out of the boot. I prayed he hadn't heard.

'Who was that talking to you?' I heard my mother shout from the foot of the staircase. 'I don't want any trouble from you, Sofia.'

'Oh, Max my neighbour just introduced himself and said that his sister is here today,' I replied anxiously. I blurted the lie out quickly, for I didn't want my parents to think that there was a man and a woman living together or having sex in the room next to mine. I was petrified that everything might end for me there and then and that they'd whisk me off back home.

'I heard exactly what Max said,' replied Mum. 'Please don't lie like that again. I think it's best if you come home every weekend from now on.' With that, she went outside to tell Dad what had happened.

I began to feel really angry and soon I was seething. I'd tried so hard with them over the past few years and here they were clamping down on me again. I'd tried to make sure that I didn't shame them and now they were punishing me once more for no reason whatsoever.

I'd signed up to sit the degree course they'd preferred, I'd never had a boyfriend, I still dressed as they wished and never wore make-up. I'd never sought help outside the family after being treated so harshly at home and I'd continued to pray every day and work hard at the weekends. I'd abided by all their rules and I thought things had got better between us because I *had* tried. Yet here I was, an 18-year-old woman on my first exciting day at university with parents who were determined to ruin my happiness with their rules.

After my parents had driven off, I put on my coat and

left the house. It was early evening and I felt the cold sea air blowing hard against my face as I wandered into the city centre. I was angry with Mum and Dad, but in the night air I soon breathed a huge sigh of relief and my anger began to subside. I remember thanking the wind for blowing my feelings of anger and entrapment away, even if only for a few moments.

I wandered excitedly down the pretty cobbled streets and the quaint lanes of Brighton and saw smiling, happy people milling around everywhere. It was the first time I was alone and had no one telling me what to do. I looked around at the new sights and sounds – it was magical. Here I was, in a place I had never been to before, on my own, wandering around like an adventurer. I decided that it was time for me to start to live my life for me. I'd tried to change things at home but it obviously wasn't working. I was still getting hurt, feeling unhappy and being restricted. Whatever I did and however much I tried, I realised that night that my parents would never change towards me – I'd always live a hellish life as long as I was attached to them.

The emotional neglect that I'd suffered from my parents was much more painful than anything else that had happened to me.

In my heart, I still wanted a mother who encouraged me and boosted me when I faced new challenges. I still wanted a mother who understood me for my failings and was happy for me to leave home, become an independent woman and make a happy, new life for herself. I wanted a mother who looked at me lovingly, who nurtured me, nourished me and loved me daily no matter where I was in the world. I also wanted a father who protected me from harm, advised me and made me feel secure. That day it became clear that, no matter how hard I tried to please my parents, they could never be the people that I wanted them to be.

I walked down to the seafront, stood on the pier and stared at the sea. It was so vast and alive but also lonely and grey. I thought for a moment that perhaps the sea thrived because it was free to come and go as it pleased. Yes, the sea also looked lonely that evening, but it was incredibly strong, powerful and courageous in its loneliness. As I stood there on the pier in my dull, grey clothes I also felt alone, but I realised that I too could feel free, strong, powerful and courageous if I really wanted to.

I pressed my hands on my wrists and thought of the scars that had been etched there over the years. I knew that I could never erase the pain I'd endured as a child, but I knew I needed to try to move on.

I realised I had to sever any emotional ties that I had with my parents. Emotionally, I buried my mother, father and uncle, along with the rest of my family. It had taken time to find the right path but, lonely and scary as it was, I knew it was the only path that could lead me to the freedom and happiness that I truly deserved.

I turned and walked back towards my new home, glad that I'd separated myself from them in my heart. Although I still craved the love a family can give, I still felt fear, but I was finally free to find and enjoy me.

I bumped into my landlord when I arrived back in the square. 'Are you off out to the Freshers' party tonight, Sofia?' he asked, smiling.

'Oh, I'm not allowed,' I answered bowing my head. It was my first night of freedom and I was on a new path of change, yet for a split second I still felt uneasy and guilty about breaking my parents' rules. But I quickly thought of the sea and the important decisions that I'd bravely made that evening. I looked up at him and smiled.

'Listen, why don't you go?' he said. 'I'll tell your mother you're asleep when she calls. You need to make friends and enjoy yourself. You have your whole life ahead of you.'

'Are you sure? Thank you, Mr Hewson,' I replied. 'Promise me that we'll keep this a secret though?'

He promised and told me I had nothing to feel guilty about. I went upstairs and sat in my bedroom. I was about to go to my first ever party, and I felt fantastic. For once, I didn't have anyone scolding me for wanting to go and enjoy myself. I went into the bathroom, ran myself a hot bath and then dressed in a pair of black leggings and a black, long-sleeved, crew-neck top. I blow-dried my hair so it was silky smooth and falling to my waist. I felt great as I looked at the end result in my bedroom mirror. My spots were much better by then and I'd also lost a bit of weight. I put on my coat and took a cab up to the university campus.

When I got out of the cab, I spotted a group of students who were heading towards the building where the party was.

'Can I go with you?' I asked a petite girl who was standing with them. She had short blonde hair and looked really friendly.

'Of course!' she said, smiling. 'I'm Amy and these are my friends. If you don't know anyone tonight just stick with us,' she added, pulling me into the group.

I tagged along, overwhelmed at how everyone constantly laughed and chatted with me.

The Freshers' Ball went on in several smaller rooms linked to a much bigger main one. At first I wandered around alone just taking it all in. Each room was filled with people and loud pumping music. One had colourful graffiti on the walls and another was filled with strobe lights and big red balloons. I looked around in awe as boys and girls mixed happily with one another, laughing, dancing and chatting.

I began dancing away, thoroughly enjoying meeting boys, girls and couples. I knew there was alcohol but I didn't want to drink because I'd never tried alcohol before and didn't think I would like it. I didn't really understand what alcohol did to people, so when I saw everyone falling around and giggling I just joined in thinking that was what people did at parties. I just let loose, danced and fell all over the place. I danced happily on the tables and chairs for hours and I hadn't touched a drop of alcohol! I had never heard music so loud before. It went right through my body and all I wanted to do was dance my socks off.

I suppose that night was the true beginning of my new life. Sometimes, I'd still feel guilty when I thought I was betraying my parents, and fearful that they'd find me out and harm me. But every time I felt guilt or fear, I tried to visualise the beautiful, free and happy sea and I'd always feel better.

The next morning I woke up feeling tired but exhilarated. It was a Friday and all I could think about was the sheer joy and liberation I'd experienced the night before. Then I remembered that I really needed to get some new clothes. I'd seen loads of girls wearing mini-skirts and halter-neck tops at the party and really wanted to dress like they did. I was free to do what I wanted now. Changing my wardrobe was the next step in my liberation!

I got dressed and walked quickly into Brighton. I didn't

have a lot of money to spend, but I went and bought my first short skirt. I'd never worn anything that revealed my legs before. I pirouetted in front of the mirror when I got back to my bedroom and felt so good. Already, I wanted to buy more skirts!

During that first month in Brighton, my previously dull, sombre and sparse wardrobe started to take on a new and vibrant shape. Within a few months, it was bulging with little skirts, brightly coloured tight tops and Wonderbras. The grey loose, baggy trousers and brown sweaters from back home were all pushed to one side and quickly forgotten – apart from when I went home at the weekends.

As well as fashion, clubbing also gripped me like a bug. After the Freshers' Ball, I'd decided to see what else was out there. I tried out Brighton clubs like The Paradox, The Escape and The Event. I particularly liked The Paradox because I was stunned by watching all the exotic dancers parade themselves on the huge, brightly lit stage. I remember hoping I'd be up there with them one day, dancing freely and happily with them.

I had never been taught how to dance like those dancers, but I had watched plenty of women dancing Bangra on TV, so put those moves into practice. Funnily enough, I was soon mimicking the dancers pretty well as I moved naturally in rhythm to the music.

It was around this time that I also decided that I wanted to feel what it was like to get tipsy. At the end of my first year at Brighton, I had my first drink in the East Slope bar at university. One evening, I walked in and they made me a 'Five Alive' – a mix of wine, cider and fruit juice – in a plastic pint glass. I sipped it slowly but it quickly made me feel relaxed and warm as I sat with a friend and got drunk.

I even told him that I loved him. I didn't, of course. It was the drink talking!

I was soon hooked on the music, the dancing and the people who socialised on the Brighton club scene, and began going out three or four times a week. Everything and everyone oozed colour and life and I simply lapped it up. I made a lot of new friends who'd take me out whenever I wanted to go clubbing. They were so full of life and always looked after me by dressing me up in sexy clothes and dancing with me all night long.

'Come on, Sofia,' they'd shriek, holding out yet another belt-like leather mini-skirt for me to wear, 'you'll look better in this.'

'Why don't you wear this glossy-red lipstick?' they'd say, as they set to work on my face.

'You look beautiful,' they'd say as we danced away together in one of our favourite Brighton haunts.

CHAPTER NINE
SEX

Despite having struck out alone, and distanced myself emotionally from my parents, I was still physically part of their lives. In accordance with my mother's rules, I had to travel home every weekend. I expected that those trips home would be difficult, and they were, especially because I was living a totally different and secret life in Brighton. But I'd promised myself to stay strong and to stick with my decisions and new path no matter how scared or guilty I felt along the way. I constantly reminded myself that I still deserved to enjoy some sort of freedom and find happiness in my life.

I also knew that, however I felt on those trips, I needed to make those two days easier for myself. During this first year at university, I continued to keep out of the house by working at Tesco. I also got a second job in Top Man in Gravesend just to keep busy. My father had bought me a second-hand car so that I could travel home at weekends and I juggled my hours so that I'd drive home on Friday nights, get up at 6am Saturday to start work at 8am at Tesco, and then work at Top Man on Sunday. I then went back to Tesco to work the evening shift before going back to my room in Brighton. I remember always feeling really tired when I got home to Gravesend on Friday nights because I'd almost always been out clubbing the night before. I didn't care, though, because being tired meant that I could just go straight to bed and not have to face anyone in my family.

When I was back in Brighton, I made sure that I always took all the necessary precautions so that my life there remained a secret. For instance, my parents would often come to Brighton unannounced just to check up on me. There was a spare room in the building and, when my parents came to see me, I would act as if the spare room was my room and put all my sensible clothes in the wardrobe in there. They never went in my real room as they assumed someone else was living in there.

I'd obviously always kept my clubbing and sexier clothes a secret from them, so I'd have an old pair of trousers and a jumper ready by my bedroom door in case I spotted their car pulling up in the street below. 'Let me see if you've got any nice new clothes, Sofia,' my mother would say, eyeing up my bedroom on one of her spontaneous visits. She'd then look through the wardrobe to see if I was still making good use of the sensible brown and grey clothes that she'd given me on the day I left home.

Although I was secretly breaking their rules by going clubbing and wearing sexier clothes and make-up, it was a completely different story when it came to boys. Yes, my parents had banned boys from my life unless there was contact through the arranged marriage process, but even at

18 I remember still not feeling particularly interested in them. I think the first problem was that I associated men with violence, but also I was far too wrapped up in so many new and exciting things to worry too much about boys. The other problem was that I didn't have a clue about boys and how to interact with them properly. I didn't know how to get a boyfriend and hadn't even kissed a boy, let alone slept with one! Put simply, there were a number of reasons why getting involved with a boy wasn't something I'd really consciously thought about, or even wanted.

However, because I seemed to be attracting male attention when I went out, I became naturally inquisitive and wanted to at least try being receptive to it. As a starting point, I decided to find out how I could 'get' a boyfriend. I remember one morning, when I'd gone back home to Gravesend and started my shift at Tesco, I asked some of the other girls how I'd know if a boy fancied me or wanted to take me out. They all laughed at my innocence, but told me that if I liked a boy I should kiss him and then invite him back to my bedroom for a coffee. 'Then you can just take it from there and see if he calls,' they said, hoping that I'd be brave enough to take my first step.

I said I'd try it, but was still unsure about it all.

One night I made my first move. It was the first time I'd ever kissed a boy. Because we were in a corner of a club, and no one could see me, I felt relaxed and was enjoying kissing him. Steve was handsome and had a nice warm smile and he made me laugh. After a while I asked him back for coffee. He accepted, looking stunned but happy. At that point I really couldn't understand why he looked so happy – it was only a coffee and perhaps more kissing, after all. We left the club together and headed back to my room in Regency Square.

'I've been tested,' Steve said, once we got back to my bedroom and were sitting on my bed.

I was already a bundle of nerves, but after he said that I didn't know what to do or say. In fact, I didn't have a clue what he was talking about. The kettle boiled away in the corner of the room and then switched itself off. The silence in the room felt really uncomfortable.

'Tested for what?' I asked, breaking the silence.

'Oh, you know. Diseases.'

'Oh, right, well, I'm glad. Did you think you were ill?' I asked him, still confused.

Steve soon realised that I was a virgin and quickly explained what he meant.

I felt so uncomfortable knowing that Steve wanted to sleep with me, and when we'd drunk the coffee he left. He didn't complain, which was nice, but after he'd gone I remember sitting on my bed feeling so silly and naive, and my parents' words kept popping into my head: 'Boys only want one thing. They will use you and dump you when they have got what they want.' So I decided that inviting men back to my room for coffee wasn't going to happen again, at least not until I was ready to go any further.

After a while, I started to see how far I could go without getting into the 'coffee' trap. I still didn't know how to get a proper boyfriend, and I didn't want to ask the Tesco girls again in case they gave me even worse advice. Instead of bringing boys home, I simply opted for the first part – meeting other guys and kissing them when I was out clubbing. I'd spot guys I fancied, go over to them, talk to them and kiss them. I started to enjoy kissing a lot more – I was soon able to kiss properly with my tongue rather than with my teeth!

Gradually, I started to feel more confident sexually, and I began asking men back to my bedroom for coffee again. We'd kiss and mess around a bit. As the kettle boiled away, I'd pull whoever it was towards me, but I still wouldn't have sex because I wasn't ready and wanted to do it with someone special.

I did have a few flashbacks about my uncle during those times, but the hardest thing to deal with was that none of the boys that I brought back seemed to want to take me on a date afterwards. It was all very confusing. I was meeting one guy every few weeks by then, but they never called to take me out again. I didn't understand why and wondered if there was something wrong with me, but now I know it was probably my nerves and inexperience, plus the fact that I wouldn't have sex with them.

I was 20 years old when I finally lost my virginity with a nice boy who, for the purpose of this book I'll call Tim Brown. Tim was a bit older than me and worked in the fish industry. He had dark hair, blue eyes and a nice body, and was so kind.

I had met Tim's sister Jane on the clubbing scene and one night we all went back to Tim's flat in Brighton. Because I trusted Jane, I felt fine with Tim and was able to get close to him. I realised that I liked him as we sat chatting around the kitchen table in their flat, and it grew into something more serious after a few weeks of us all spending time together.

I felt ready to have sex with Tim because he seemed so keen and had even asked to take me out, so after our second date we tried to have sex in his single bed. It was really daunting. I felt so nervous that I told him to stop each time we got close to penetration. The whole thing went on all night and I remember us still trying when the postman turned up in the morning!

But Tim was really patient with me, the poor thing – it took us three weeks to get there! I was pleased that I'd waited until I'd met a boy like him.

When it finally happened, I burst out crying because I felt a huge wave of relief surging through me. I didn't feel confused or sad; I felt as free and as happy as a bird. I'd feared sex so much because of my past, yet it was magical when I finally did it. I felt like I'd really found my femininity.

Tim and I dated for three months but eventually we parted because he didn't like it that I was still going out partying three or four nights a week. The problem was that I didn't understand you couldn't do that in relationships. I was still inexperienced and naive, and didn't have a clue what being with someone was all about. I did love Tim but I couldn't fit in all the other enjoyable things in my life.

But straight after Tim, I met another man.

I was enjoying a night out at The Paradox club when I first spotted him. I was sitting at a table near the dance floor when I noticed a man standing alone at the bar. He looked exactly like a movie star, and was looking straight at me, smiling. I noticed his smart dark suit and his sexy dark hair. After a few minutes of us staring at one another, he sent me over a drink, and I smiled at him.

I felt confident that night, and I felt that I looked good. I was wearing a black playsuit dress (a dress which has shorts rather than a skirt) that I'd made out of another dress and cleverly safety-pinned together between my legs. My hair was down and I was wearing my only pair of black patent clubbing heels. After the drink arrived, I went over to the bar, thanked him and introduced myself, fluttering my eyelashes as fast as I could. He was so gorgeous. Let's call him Peter, which is not his real name.

'It's such a pleasure to meet you,' he said. 'I've seen you in here before, but tonight you look especially beautiful so I couldn't resist sending you over something to drink.'

We spent the night chatting about what we did and where we liked going out in Brighton. We kissed at the end of the night, and when I gave him my number he asked me for dinner the following night. We went to a fantastic Japanese restaurant in Brighton for our first date, and got on really well. Peter's job wasn't tremendously well paid, so wasn't flush, but it didn't matter to me – he seemed so kind and genuine.

Peter dropped me off at the house after we'd eaten. 'I really want to see you again, but I need to take things slowly,' he said. 'I've been hurt before and don't want to rush.'

'Of course,' I said, pleased that he was so refreshingly honest. 'Why don't you come round on Wednesday? Perhaps we can go clubbing.'

When he agreed, I kissed him goodnight and literally skipped up to my bedroom. I couldn't wait to see him again. He seemed shy and vulnerable and that made me want to care for and protect him. In fact, it made me want to love him. Also great was that he seemed interested in me as a person, not just sexually. Our clubbing date was fantastic – I enjoyed his company and the fact that he didn't push to get me into bed. As we got to know each other, it became clear that sex would come when I was ready. For the moment, we were happy becoming boyfriend and girlfriend.

The sex came a few months later. Peter was experimental

in bed and I started to try new things out with him. Some nights, though, Peter would be quite rough in bed. I wasn't entirely comfortable, but accepted it – at that point I just wanted to please and care for him. It didn't hurt – and I didn't know any different anyway – so I felt it was fine to continue as we were.

We did romantic things, too. Peter loved the open space and the thrill of having sex in the open, so we'd often drive off into the country and make love outdoors or in the car. We were always careful that no one could see us and we always went to secluded spots. Aside from our experimental sex life, the relationship was very natural and low key, and I can see why I loved Peter in the beginning.

Sadly, the cracks started to show within a year.

What had brought us together eventually tore us apart. Peter and I loved clubbing together, and still went every Wednesday or Thursday night. We always had a great time, but one night Peter revealed a side to him that I had not seen before. We were dancing away in a small local disco when Peter lashed out and punched another man in the face.

'What did you do that for?' I screamed, as the man lay unconscious on the dance floor. 'What have you done?'

'He was staring at you. He deserved it,' Peter shouted, glaring at me.

Tears rolled down my cheeks. I was so shocked. Peter had never been violent, yet had suddenly exploded like a volcano right in front of me, knocking a man out cold. I ran off to the toilet, crying. When I came out, Peter said we were leaving and that the man was fine. He'd calmed down and seemed apologetic, but I couldn't get that scene out of my head. I'd never seen aggression in Peter, and it worried me.

I tried to put the nightclub incident to the back of my mind, but a week later I was cleaning Peter's kitchen floor when he exploded again. I'd thrown a bucket of soapy water on to his patio and he lost it.

'You f***ing Paki,' Peter shouted. 'Is that what you do in Pakistan?' He came at me and threw me on to the stairs.

I was terrified and crying, 'I'm sorry, Peter, it won't happen again.'

Then something happened that I did not expect. He put his hands around my neck and started to squeeze. I could feel the pressure building up in my head, as if it was about to burst. 'I can't breathe, please let me go. I can't breathe!'

He looked at me for a second and then released his grip. 'Go and clean that up. Mop it up now,' he yelled, and stormed out into the garden.

Unfortunately, at the time, in my weak state, I still wanted his love so would often ask Peter what I could do to make him love me.

'There's only one thing you can do,' Peter told me one day. 'I find it hard to trust women and the only way we can build some trust between us is if you get pregnant.'

My mouth dropped open in shock.

I wasn't even married and he wanted me to have a child! My family didn't even know that I had a boyfriend. I'd managed to conceal my new life from my parents thus far, but this was something totally different. I didn't even want to begin to imagine what they would say to me if they found out. But Peter was persistent and, having had so much pain in my life, I was desperate for love. Looking back, it seems so obvious that I was clinging on to something that was obviously wrong.

That month I stopped using contraception and, after a

few weeks, I fell pregnant. I did four tests and they were all positive. As I watched the blue line seep across the window, I was shocked and afraid but also relieved. I took the test to show Peter at his work and, when I told him the news, his eyes lit up. 'Now we can be a proper family,' he said, as he hugged me.

Over the next few weeks, I kept myself busy and healthy. I knew that I would have to deal with my parents eventually but for the moment all I wanted to focus on was my unborn child. Little did I know that Peter had yet another shock in store for me.

A month later, he made a confession. He told me that he already had a child and he suddenly didn't feel ready to bring another child into the world. In short, he'd booked me into an abortion clinic and paid for the procedure already.

I was totally numb, and couldn't even muster any tears. I just sat there, emotionless and dumbfounded. Running around in circles after this man seemed to have got me nowhere – I was completely exhausted and drained.

Peter took me to the clinic and, when my name was called to see the counsellor, he took my hand and told me he'd be there when I came out. The counsellor explained to me that they needed me to be certain that I was doing the right thing before they performed the procedure. Up until this point, I'd managed to hold it together but suddenly I was pouring my heart out, telling him that having a baby hadn't even been my choice in the first place and neither was the decision to have an abortion.

I went back to where Peter was waiting and he could see that I'd been crying. When he found out that I'd told the counsellor the whole story, he was furious and stormed out, leaving me to deal with the rest of the appointment on my own.

Later that day, the doctors discovered that my pregnancy was, in fact, ectopic. I needed to be operated on and, because there was a certain amount of risk involved in the procedure, the doctors told me I should let someone know what was happening. I tried to call Peter but could not get through to him.

After numerous failed attempts, in desperation, I called Tim Brown's mother. I explained what was happening to me and I asked her if she would pray for me. In this situation, the first call most women would make would be to their family but I couldn't call mine as they had no idea what was going on, and I just couldn't tell them – the shame would have been too great.

A few hours later, Tim's mother and his sisters turned up at the hospital with flowers and magazines. I'll never forget their kindness – they were the only people who I felt able to turn to at that terrible time. Peter eventually turned up once I had come round from the operation. When he walked in, I had only just woken up and was in too much pain to worry about why he had not been there earlier.

The operation was a success. The doctors had told me that there was a risk of losing my ovaries during the procedure but, thankfully, this didn't happen and I hope that in the future God will bless me with a child to love.

A priest visited me while I was recovering and we decided to name the baby as a healing process. I named him Frances – which means Freedom. Hopefully, Frances is free and his spirit is finally happy.

I needed two weeks' bed rest after the operation. Peter had told me he couldn't look after me, so I had to call my mother. I could barely walk and had told her that I'd had a cyst removed and needed someone to look after me while I recuperated. I asked her if she could come and fetch me, and she came straight away. In fact, she spent two weeks nursing me back to health at home. Although most of that period was a bit of a blur, I know that she looked after me really well. I felt terrible that I had to lie to her, but, if she'd known the truth, she would have been mortified. Mum, I'm sorry I had to lie but I didn't want to bring shame and disrespect to the family.

After a few weeks, I was well enough to return to Peter (or my landlord, as my parents knew him). I went back to university and was excused from my exams. I told myself that Peter would change and look after me after all that I had been through for him.

Sadly, things didn't improve. It was nearly Christmas and he had promised that we would spend the festive period together. I had even lied to my parents and said that I had a lot of work to catch up on and would have to stay in Brighton to finish it.

'I can't wait, Sofia,' he said, smiling as he hugged me tightly. 'We'll be able to wake up together and open our presents in bed.' But two days beforehand, Peter suddenly changed his mind and told me that he was going to his mother's for Christmas instead. 'We'll celebrate on Boxing Day. How does that sound?' Peter had said, but I knew in my heart that something just wasn't right.

I went home to my family feeling quite uneasy and sad. We didn't celebrate Christmas anyway but, as there wasn't anyone else in Brighton, it was really my only option. I called Tesco and offered to work there if they needed me to and then on Boxing Day I drove back to Brighton early. It was only after I had laid Peter's presents under the tree that I found a note from him on his bed saying he was staying at his mother's for another day. I panicked and called his mum but she said that he wasn't there. I felt sick and angry, so just packed my things and left there and then. It turned out that he had been seeing someone else behind my back. Peter was a liar and there are three things I will never want in my life and that's a liar, a cheat or a thief. It's black and white to me.

Looking back, Peter was the worst thing that could have happened to me. My first real love had let me down, had lied and was violent. I wasn't able to make love to a man for a long time afterwards – I was way too frightened of having my heart broken again and of loving someone who might turn violent or be unfaithful.

I felt so low after the break-up but, as we all do, I tried to get over it and move on. Sadly, though, it took me almost a decade to trust a man and fall in love again. I tried not to hang on to the past, but the memories of my father, my uncle and Peter were so painful and lingering.

After breaking up with Peter, I decided to make a few changes. I knew that what I needed most of all was something to look forward to. After injecting so much energy into a failed relationship, I knew it was time to focus on doing things for me again.

I found a new flat share in Brighton with two other male students (I told my parents they were gay as they felt it was acceptable for me to live with gay men) and settled in quickly. Now I had time to think long and hard about my career. I hadn't been enjoying the Biology and Management course, as I'd only really chosen the course to please my parents, so I decided to take a year out and not tell them. I applied to Brighton University to do what I really wanted: Performing Arts.

I opted for the year out because I wanted to change courses at university – I'd only studied Biology to keep my parents happy. What I desperately wanted to do was to study performing arts. The year out enabled me to earn some money so that I could change to the course I really wanted to do. I'd never had enough money coming in from my parents, and I wanted to be financially independent from them. Money meant freedom.

I got a job with Legal and General taking incoming calls and dealing with dissatisfied customers, and excelled because of the customer service skills that I luckily seemed to have – I found it easy to chat with people and enjoyed sorting out their problems.

Then, for a bit of light relief, I started working as Sammy The Sea Lion at the Sealife Centre on Brighton Pier every other Saturday. I remember telling my parents I had exams to study for so couldn't come home every weekend. Little did they know I was getting up early every other Saturday and heading down to the seafront with a big grey fluffy costume tucked under my arm. I loved it.

The job involved dressing up in the suit and greeting all the kids as they arrived at the Sealife Centre. I loved watching all the kids' eyes light up when they saw me waving at them from the entrance door. They'd skip up to me and ask me hundreds of questions. I hugged and played with as many of them as I could until I was exhausted. I loved giving my all to those kids, as they embraced my affection and reciprocated it so naturally.

To top my money up, I also got a night job at The

Paradox club. The manager had approached me after watching me dancing and offered me a job as a dancer. I could hardly believe my luck. I started dancing on stage, and it felt like a dream come true. Ever since my first ever night out at The Paradox club, I'd always wanted to get up on the stage and dance with all the other girls.

On my first shift, I was proud but nervous. I got changed in the little staff room at the back of the club, putting on a big Afro wig, black hot pants and a bright-green funky top! Then I climbed on to the stage with all the other dancers and got stuck in. I loved the crowd looking up and smiling at me – they seemed to love what I was doing. I was happiest in the dancing job. Not only was I immersed in the sound of music, but I was also entertaining people. I felt like I'd felt when I'd performed in the plays at my junior school.

I made some really good friends on my course, such as Kamran, who was both Muslim and gay; and George who was Indian, and also gay – other students who, like me, were Asian and had secret lives. I was surrounded by people whose creativity and true identity had been suppressed by their cultures – now here they were, expressing themselves freely through their chosen art form. It was comforting to know that there were others in the same boat as me.

This was the first time I'd really had a voice and was allowed to sing and act to my heart's content – and be praised for it! It was all so new to me and of course my parents had no idea that I had changed course – they still thought I was studying science.

Despite it being shrouded in secrecy, life was good. I finally had a decent amount of money in my pocket, and after a few months I began to forget about Peter. The smile was well and truly back on my face. From time to time I still felt guilty about lying to my parents, but I knew that keeping things a secret was the safest way for me. Living my life that way gave me a shot at being truly happy. And, slowly but surely, I was getting there.

Little did I know that things were about to take a shocking turn for the worse. My happiness was about to be struck down in a flash.

CHAPTER TEN

KIDNAPPED

It was a cold night, the sea air was harsher than normal. I'd been out dancing at The Paradox and had been dropped home by Mumin, a Palestinian friend who had become like a brother to me. The wind was ripping through my coat as I walked up towards the front door. I was wearing a low-cut top and a short skirt, and was shaking with cold as I put the key in the lock.

But when I turned the key I froze. My mother was standing there by the door in the darkness. It frightened the life out of me.

'What are you doing here?' I said in complete shock.

Without saying a word my mother moved between me and the front door, blocking my way in. I knew that something terrible was about to happen. I was so scared. My mother looked so angry, and I suddenly felt ashamed of the way I was dressed. I tried to conceal my clothes under my winter coat.

'You're coming home right now,' she screamed, her face

reddening with fury. 'You're leaving Brighton and you can't ever come back. I know what you're up to, young lady.'

I then spotted my flatmate Oliver who was standing in his pyjamas at the top of the staircase. My mother's bellowing voice had woken him up but I didn't want him to get involved.

'Go back to bed, Oliver,' I said. 'I'm fine. I'll ring you tomorrow.'

There was no point in trying to get help from Oliver. I'd seen the threatening look in my mother's eyes, and knew she meant business. There was nothing to do but to go with her: I was terrified of her and of what might happen to me if I didn't do what she told me to do. I'd heard stories of girls who had been taken from their homes and married off in Pakistan and India. I knew that honour killings happened and, ever since I was a child, my father had told me that I might be killed if I dishonoured the family name. I felt I had no choice – I was truly frightened for my life.

As well as fear, I was filled with an overwhelming sense of guilt and shame. Standing there facing my mother in my skimpy top and mini-skirt, I felt that she was justified in her actions and that I did need to be punished. All the tireless emotional and practical work that I'd done to change my life and find happiness was suddenly undone as the power of my family's distorted view of our culture completely took over my mind. I looked down at my black patent heels and red-painted nails, and felt crushed. Looking back, that moment of powerlessness only proved how much 'honour' was ingrained in me. In a few moments of weakness and fear, I'd lost everything to it and had given up my journey to freedom.

Then, to my horror, my brother Majid appeared in the doorway. Majid was tall and strong and I knew he was there in case I needed to be manhandled out of my flat. I felt submissive, helpless and drowned in fear and shame. I was shaking as I tried to ask my mother how she knew about my nights at the Paradox.

'Get your things, Sofia, and come with us,' was all she said.

I walked upstairs to my room feeling completely defeated.

As I followed my mother and Majid down to their car, I felt like my life was well and truly over. I noticed my sister Tahira was also in the car – she sat in silence, just looking at me. My mother snarled at me to get into the car and keep quiet. Majid bundled me into the back seat, and she slammed the door. I noticed Majid put something in the glove compartment, but couldn't really see what it was.

We drove back to Kent in silence.

My head was clouded with disappointment, fear and guilt. I was lost and trapped and had no idea what to do. I started to cry as we approached Gravesend and, as the tears rolled down my face, I thought that it was the end for me in Brighton and that my flight to freedom was completely doomed.

'You're not going back to university, Sofia,' said my mother as we stopped outside the house. 'It's over. You need to be a good Muslim girl and stay at home with us.'

It was almost dawn. I was drained.

My mother warmed slightly when we got in – she was pleased with herself for bringing her shameful daughter back home. 'I'll look after you from now on, Sofia,' she said, holding me by the hand and leading me into the kitchen. 'All you need to do is stay here and do as I say. Then you won't come to any harm.

She must have seen the fear and pain etched on my face, because she reached out and put her hand on my shoulder. I noticed a glimmer of guilt in her eyes as she looked into mine. In that moment of tenderness I knew my mother felt she had no choice but to shackle her daughter within the confines of her own home.

Majid walked slowly into the kitchen. He was holding a carving knife. I started to tremble in fear. 'What's that knife for?' I said, bursting into tears. 'Are you going to kill me? Please don't harm me. I'll do whatever you say. Please, Mum, don't use the knife...'

I cried out in terror as Mum took her hand off my shoulder. 'Put the knife back in the drawer, Majid, and go to bed,' she said calmly. 'It's finished now. Sofia is back where she belongs and will stay downstairs in the cellar. Everything's going to be fine.'

My parents had converted the cellar space into a bedroom – it was still a little damp and I had a few spiders for company, but it was nice enough.

Majid wandered off upstairs to his room. I discovered later that it was the carving knife that had been in the glove compartment on the journey back to Kent. Years later, to my horror, I learned from Tahira that my mother's intention had been to kill me if I'd put up a fight and disobeyed her, though I doubt if she could have gone through with it.

Over the next few days, I felt like I was living under house arrest as I stayed fearfully in the confines of the cellar. I ate alone and the days and nights merged into one. I only slept when sleep came to me. I was restless and anxious with memories of the night my mother had kidnapped me, and in my darkest hour I remember wanting to die.

As I lay in my dark, damp room, thinking of where and who I was, I remembered what I'd been told about Gravesend. Gravesend is the place where the last victims of the Plague were buried. For me it had always been a dead-end place, but, as time passed in the cellar, I knew that I couldn't let that place become the last stop for me.

After a week or so, I began to clear my mind and was able to focus on my life and future again. I would lie on the bed in the cellar and think of how vast and beautiful the sea had been the night I'd stood alone on Brighton pier when I started university. During those moments, I knew that I couldn't and wouldn't give up.

I began making tentative plans to escape.

A few weeks into my ordeal, I plucked up the courage to ask my mother if I could go back to work at Tesco. All I knew was that getting out of the house might provide me with the right opportunity to get away.

'I'll work hard every day and do everything that you need me to,' I begged her one morning.

Mum agreed to let me go. 'But you'll have to be watched over by Majid for a while until we can trust you again,' she warned.

Under strict surveillance I began shifting again at Tesco. My brother or my mother would chaperone me every day, and if I needed anything from the shops then someone else in the family went out to get it for me. I cleverly slotted myself back into the old family routine, though, by doing everything that I was told. I'd get up at sunrise, dress in the old clothes my mother had given me and go up to the living room to pray with my family before breakfast. Then I'd walk to Tesco with either Majid or my mother.

My days were spent stacking shelves and stocktaking. I kept myself to myself and dreaded the end of the shift when my mother or Majid would be outside waiting to take me home. The routine was simple and boring, but I stuck with it. I never spoke at any length with my family – the only time they heard my voice was when I prayed or asked for something from the shops. No one knew what was going on in my heart and head. Although I was focusing hard on finding an exit, that month was still a living hell.

I made a friend at Tesco who soon became a very bright light in my dour depressing life. He would turn out to be the exit I needed. I really believe that God sent him to me to free me. No matter how painful life had become, I still believed that God was always watching over me during my bleakest hours at night in the cellar.

Graham was tall, handsome, dark and quiet. He worked in the bakery and I'd quickly warmed to him. I knew he wasn't in cahoots with my family and so I knew that I could trust him. I was often hungry after work, so Graham and I would sneak into the back of the shop and gobble up any leftovers from the bakery.

Eating cakes with Graham was the one thing that brought a smile to my face during this time. I loved those 15-minute windows when Graham would wink at me as I stood by the counter at the end of our shift. I'd then rush into the back room behind the oven with him.

Over the weeks, we got to know each other, but I didn't tell him the full story about my situation at home. I simply said I was back from Brighton for a while. Despite this, Graham began to notice I looked troubled.

'I've just bought a car,' he said one day, smiling. 'I'd love to take you out in it. It might do you some good. You really look like you need a day out, Sofia. I can see something is bothering you.'

'It's a long story,' I replied. 'One day I'll tell you. But, yes, I'd love a trip in your new car.'

I knew then that Graham was sensitive and that he cared about me, but I still wasn't ready to open up to him just yet.

A few weeks passed, before I felt safe to talk to him. I suggested we went for a drive one lunchtime, but said I had to make sure I couldn't be seen. Graham suggested I hid on the floor of his Ford Capri, and off we went.

Even though we only drove around for 20 minutes, I felt so free crouching there by the passenger seat. Finally I could breathe again, and it was bliss. I wasn't at Tesco, where there were other Asians constantly watching over me, and I wasn't in the stifling cellar room with my family upstairs listening to my every move. It was wonderful to be in a new space with a new and friendly face by my side.

I told Graham the whole story as we drove around Strood. Graham was amazing. He offered to call Legal & General to tell them I was OK, and better still he said he would drive me back to Brighton. 'I think you should carry on fighting,' he said as we pulled up in a side road next to Tesco.

'Thanks, Graham,' I said, handing him my boss's phone number. 'You're right. I just need a bit more time.'

I was so relieved that there was someone in my life who I could trust again. As I walked back to work, I knew that Graham had been sent to save me. I finally had the opportunity that I needed. It was only a matter of days before I was ready to take the plunge.

'Can we go today at lunchtime?' I asked Graham one Saturday morning. I hardly had any possessions at my parents' house (all my stuff was still in Brighton), so I'd shoved the few things I did have in a carrier bag and taken it to work with me. I knew that Saturday would provide the best opportunity to escape unnoticed because it was always one of the busiest days at the store. In addition, my parents and siblings were normally all out working on Saturdays. 'I've told Mum that I finish at 2pm today, so, if we go at midday, no one will be waiting to collect me.'

Graham nodded. He wasn't bothered about being implicated or missing the afternoon shift at work. It was much more important for him to help me out.

The morning shift was over. I grabbed my bag and left the building. My heart was pounding when I saw Graham sitting calmly in his Capri. I looked around to make sure that no one was watching, dashed over and climbed in. It was only a few months since my mother had kidnapped me, and I was pretty scared as I ducked down on to the floor and slammed the door behind me. Graham promptly started the engine. As I crouched down by the glove compartment clutching my bag, I couldn't wait for Graham to drive off.

'You'll be fine, Sofia,' he said. 'Let's go back to your old flat and decide what to do after that.'

It wasn't until we got on to the motorway that I felt safe enough to get up from the floor. I took a deep breath and moved into the passenger seat. I looked around in case my family was following us. I knew how switched on my parents were and I couldn't take any chances. But there was no sign of them.

It was strange seeing my old flat again, but I was so

relieved to be back. However, my relief was short lived. Oliver came out of his bedroom and confirmed my worst fears.

'Your mum has called,' he said. 'She's on your tail. You need to get out of here. She said she'll be here in five minutes.'

'OK,' I said. 'Please don't tell here anything when she turns up. I'll call you soon.' With that, we left.

There was no way I was going to get caught by my mother again. I would do whatever it took to escape my family and never go back to the cellar. My life meant more to me than ever now.

I hurried back to Graham's car, curled my body into a tight ball, and we sped off.

CHAPTER ELEVEN

HONOUR KILLING

I knew that I had to move so that my mother wouldn't be able to find me. I wanted to go to the other side of town so that I could live close to a guy I knew. I'll call him Omar, which is not his real name. Although we weren't close, Omar was always discreet; he was also tall and confident, so I'd always felt protected whenever I was around him.

I was so scared. During the first week at my new place, I'd jump whenever I heard a car door slam in the street. I'd fret that my mother might somehow manage to find me. If she did, there was a chance I'd come to some serious harm. Despite my fear, I'd also reached a turning point – the guilt that I'd carried with me for so long had suddenly vanished.

I didn't feel an iota of guilt about running away from my parents – they'd caused me too much pain by then. Being imprisoned in the basement room and seeing my brother holding the carving knife in the kitchen had been the final straw.

I had got back to Brighton in time for the start of my

new Performing Arts degree course, but had to think long and hard about going back to university. I felt it might be too dangerous, but as the weeks drifted by I decided I wanted to take the chance. I was desperate to take my degree course. I also needed to earn money, so I opted to work the odd day shift at Legal & General too.

I am still in touch with Kamran, one of my best friends from university, and he said he remembered when I went missing from Brighton University for a month and everyone wondered where I was. Little did they know how much danger I was in.

Autumn term started. I made sure that I kept a low profile wherever I was, and that I was always covered up properly. I'd wear a blue baseball jacket and matching baseball cap, and clothes that I knew my mother wouldn't recognise me in.

I felt fine wandering around on the campus every day because it wasn't on the site that my parents were familiar with, but I sometimes felt afraid when I walked the long route from my new flat and up to the university. I'd hold my new mobile phone tightly, constantly look over my shoulder and pray that God was protecting me.

One evening, as I was sitting on the floor of my bedroom sorting out my clothes, there was a knock at the front door.

I let Omar into the house and he followed me into my room and hovered near the door. He had the air of someone who wanted to confess something and was trying to summon up the courage to do so.

'I've got deep feelings for you, Sofia,' Omar finally said coyly. 'It's eating me up at the moment and I really don't know what to do. Do you feel anything for me? Please tell me you do.'

I think Omar's direct approach was helped by the fact that he'd obviously had a couple of drinks before coming to speak to me.

He spoke calmly and politely, but I remember feeling completely shocked and unsure of what to say. Omar was like a brother to me.

'Let's chat another time, Omar,' I said calmly. 'I've got exams this week, let's talk at the weekend.'

As I spoke, I noticed Omar's face changing. He looked angry and it scared me.

I woke early the next morning and sleepily checked my mobile phone. I always kept it on silent under my pillow, and, after Omar's confession the night before, I was glad to have it with me.

Someone had sent me a text message: 'Mum is sending someone to kill you. She's hired a hit man. He'll find you. You need to disappear for a bit. Saira xx'.

I was horrified. Saira's words seemed so extreme that I could hardly believe this was happening. But the more I thought about it, the more I came to believe that an honour killing was a distinct possibility. It would have become the final option for my parents. They wanted their ordeal to be over. This was the solution.

I began to shake with fear, then jumped out of bed and flew into action. I'd faced death a few months ago in the kitchen, and I knew full well that it was once again close. I didn't even think about going to the police at that point, but I needed to tell someone. I decided to tell Omar. As he had been looking after me, I thought it only right that he knew what was going on in my life. Within minutes, I was dressed and over at Omar's place, where he was eating breakfast.

'I need to tell you something, Omar,' I said quietly. 'You know that I've had a lot of trouble with my family. The trouble now is that my mother wants to kill me. It sounds farfetched, but it's true. I'm telling you because I don't want to put your life in jeopardy. I also need your advice and help. I think I should leave now, but you mustn't ever tell anyone you know where I am or that I was here.'

I finished and looked straight at him, waiting for his response. To my amazement, Omar just stared at me blankly. He didn't seem shocked or surprised at all.

After a few moments, he spoke. 'It's fine, Sofia,' he said calmly. 'I understand, I'll be careful. If anyone stops by asking for you or calls me, I'll pretend that I've never seen or heard of you. If you need food or anything, I'll go and get it for you.'

With that, he cleared his breakfast things from the table and told me he was leaving for work.

It had been an odd exchange, but nevertheless I was relieved that I had his support. I called in sick at Legal & General and at university, and then spent the next ten days holed up in my bedroom. I felt trapped and still worried about Omar's intentions after he had made that pass at me, but my safety was my priority. I simply had to stay put.

I was terrified and every time I heard a voice outside, or a car door slam, I thought it was someone who had been sent to kill me. I gave Omar the little money I had left in my bank account and he would often cook food for me. He didn't come on to me again, but sometimes turned up at my place drunk and wanted to see me for a chat.

When I hadn't heard from my sister again for a while, I finally felt confident enough to go out and get some fresh air. I'd been longing to be outside again and just couldn't face being cooped up any longer. I wrapped up warm and put a cap on to hide my face. With my heart in my mouth, I walked to the end of the road. I could see the seafront. After nearly a fortnight of isolation, I enjoyed standing there taking in the fresh, crisp sea air. I felt better as I walked back into my flat.

Later on, I went round to Omar's house and one of his housemates let me in. Omar mustn't have realised I was there and, when I walked into the lounge, he was sitting on the sofa talking quietly on the phone. He put the phone down as soon as he spotted me in the doorway, telling whoever was on the line that he had to go. His behaviour seemed strange, but I told myself that my paranoia was probably distorting things and went home to bed and thought nothing more of it.

My suspicions about Omar were further aroused the next night when he told me that I had to leave the place where I was living. 'You're in danger,' he said sternly. 'Your mother contacted me yesterday and she's coming up to Brighton. I didn't say where you were but she said she wanted to meet me.'

'How did she contact you? It's impossible that she knows to call you. Have you contacted her?' I began to shake and my heart began to pound.

'No, but a Muslim man came round to the flat the other night. He asked about you. I was frightened of him so I couldn't lie. They must've found my number.'

Omar said he was sorry, and that he thought the man might have been a hitman. But he reassured me that he did not tell him where I was. Omar looked scared too.

'You need to leave,' he said. 'I think he's coming back at the weekend to ask more questions. I don't know what to make of it all.'

Not wanting to waste another second, I went home and packed my things. I was confused about what Omar had said – it didn't make any sense. As I finished clearing my desk, I noticed that my personal organiser had been moved. It was in the wrong drawer. I was always so careful with my organiser because I knew that it contained many personal names and phone numbers. If ever my mother had ever found it, she would have been able to track me down in a second.

I froze. Omar was the only person who had been in my room. He must have found the organiser, gone through it and perhaps contacted my mother himself. She must have then sent one of my brothers or another family member to kill me. Maybe Omar had called her because he was upset that I hadn't wanted to date him. Perhaps his warning for me to get out had been given out of guilt.

My thoughts were all over the place. Whatever had happened, my life was in danger and I needed to take action. I went straight into survival mode. I grabbed my bag, left my rent on the bedside table, and left quietly. I didn't say goodbye to Omar.

Once outside, I called my Salsa teacher. I'd met Joaquin at Orianna's club in Brighton that summer. He was short and muscly with olive skin, and had been a good friend to me. He was the only other person I'd ever trusted in Brighton, and I knew that he'd help me.

I felt really vulnerable when I arrived at his flat. Joaquin sat me down and I explained what had happened. Straight away, he told me that my only option was to contact the police. 'You need to take your mobile phone to the police and show them your sister's text right now. I'll go with you,' he said, hugging me tightly.

Above left: As a small child, unaware of the twists and turns – both good and bad – my life was to take in future years.

Above right: I was very young when I first became bitten by the acting bug. Here I am aged six in a school Christmas play.

Below left: Underneath the smile was an unhappy girl. I was twelve when this photo was taken and desperately insecure.

Below right: In the garden at Northcote Road – I made that dress myself!

Above left: In this play, my part was that of a stuck-up, man-eating rich girl. A good thing I can act, as this was a far cry from my real life!

Above right: I've always loved to write music. This photograph shows me playing a devil in a musical I wrote called *Life After Death*. As well as writing and performing in it, I did all the choreography and direction. Not bad for a 17-year-old.

Below left: Finally free! A night out at university in Brighton – it wasn't long before my parents found out about my new lifestyle there …

Below right: I really relished my new freedom – here I am out clubbing.

The photos above and below left were taken before my nose job; the photo below right shows me after the operation.

I really threw myself into performance once I was away from my parents' rules, plus I was also pretty enterprising when it came to making ends meet.

Above: My dance company, Provocative Promotions.

Below left: I was also the lead singer in a gay band and sang at gay venues.

Below right: Some time off with a couple of my friends who were drag queens down in Brighton. The one on the right is Grace.

Above: Me, Rebecca and Amra. The three of us formed the second incarnation of Sugar Brown. We had a number six hit on MTV Base.

Below left: With Kamran Sarwa, my best friend from university. He's now a successful designer.

Below right: My beloved Daphne, whose wisdom and love taught me so much.

I'm invited to a lot of red carpet events and love socialising at them. Sometimes I'm lucky enough to meet some of the stars of the films.

Above: With the delightful Will Smith.

Below left: Having a laugh with Colin Farrell. Luckily he didn't mind my cheeky question when I interviewed him for Zee TV on the red carpet!
© *Getty Images*

Below right: At the Cartier Polo event in Windsor Great Park with Jimmy Choo, the man behind the most fabulous shoes in the world, and John Stevens.
© *Getty Images*

Above: A still from one of my films, *Cash and Curry*.

Below: In Mumbai for Channel 4's *Bollywood Star*. *L–R* Saydur Rahman, me, Rivonia Essop and Ricky Verdee.

Above: Entertaining the Gurkhas.

Below left: With my very great friend Federica – it was Federica who introduced me to the love of my life, Fabrizio.

Below right: With my gorgeous dog, Daphne.

Having had to deal with a lot of tough issues in my life, I'm now where I want to be. I'm with the man I love and fulfilling my dreams as an actress, model and signer. But I'll never forget the past and hope to help young women who are having similar problems to the ones I went through.

Joaquin was amazed that I hadn't gone to the police already. But getting help from an authority in the outside world had never been an option in the past, and I still hadn't felt it was.

It was close to midnight when we left Joaquin's flat and got a taxi to Hove police station. When we arrived, I was told to sit down in a tiny, sparsely furnished room where the police asked me to tell them my story. At first, I was so scared that I couldn't even speak. I knew that Joaquin was waiting outside, but, because I was sitting all alone with a couple of strangers in a small, unfamiliar room, I only felt able to start when the policemen promised me that I was doing the right thing.

I told them the whole story from beginning to end. I explained how trapped and mistreated I'd been as a child, how I'd started to live a double life in Brighton, and why my mother had kidnapped me. I told them about the knife that my brother had held in the kitchen, and about me living in the cellar. And I then showed them my sister's text.

I felt worried that the policemen would laugh off my allegations. After all, saying that her mother wanted her dead was a shocking claim for a young girl to make. I was scared of sounding ridiculous, but, as the policemen sat back and listened while taking copious notes, I came to believe that they understood and would help me.

'We understand, Sofia,' said one of the policemen. 'We're not going to take any risks with this. I need to take your formal statement and then find you some protection. I'll also need to send someone to go and speak to your mother.'

Once I'd given my statement, I was terrified. I'd finally told everything to someone outside the family, and I could feel the honour that my parents had drummed into my head for so many years trying to challenge, create fear and weaken me again.

The police said that they would contact my mother and warn her not to approach me. They took out an injunction against her and told her that, if I called them to say she had come near me, they would arrest her. I think this frightened my mother and she promised not to contact me again. They also gave me a special number that I could ring if I felt I was in any danger. I finally started to feel a bit more secure – at least something had been done and I felt like someone was looking out for me.

I did exactly as the police had said: I called my year tutor at university and my manager at Legal & General. They were always so great with me, even after I'd failed to show up at work. Legal & General had made a note of Graham's information when he'd called them, and had even held my position open.

The following Monday, I went in to work my first shift. I explained to my manager that I was under police protection and that he was not to put any calls through to me or tell my family that I was working there. I didn't explain exactly what had happened, but assured him that, so long as he did as I asked, I'd be fine. He was wonderful about it, and said he understood completely – even though he looked a bit surprised! I thanked him before going to sit quietly at my desk.

I took a handful of the usual calls, though whenever the phone rang I felt nauseous and prayed that it wasn't my mother. However, as more and more calls came in, I began to feel stronger and more confident that I didn't need to worry. I eventually managed to blank my mother's face from my mind.

Not that I wasn't still fearful. Every evening and morning I'd walk to and from work or university and feel paranoid that someone was behind or watching me. I'd walk so fast that I'd often arrive feeling really flustered and afraid. But I felt better when the police first updated me with their plans.

A few days after I'd made my statement, the police told me that they'd gone to see my mother and told her to stay away from me. They also told her that they knew exactly what had happened within our family. I didn't ask what my mother had said or what had been agreed, but I felt safe knowing that my mother wouldn't ever cross the line again. If anything happened to me, then the finger would most definitely be pointed at her.

Time heals all wounds, as they say, and as the weeks went by I gradually started to find my feet again – I'd even started to wear my normal clothes. Every day, I felt as if 'Sofia' was slowly but surely coming back, and I did all I could to keep moving on.

The only people I chatted to during this period were my work colleagues and some of the students who I'd met on my new course. Then there was Joaquin, who I was staying with. As for everyone else, I had to cut them all off for fear of them getting into trouble with my family. Also, there was the fear that they would contact my family.

It was a challenging time, but I drew so much strength out of it and pulled through. I'm so proud of myself for coping and battling on back then. It felt so good to know that I was managing and not becoming weakened under pressure. My positive attitude, together with protection I was getting from the police, made me feel braver.

After several weeks had passed, my old flatmate Oliver

called my mobile. He told me that my mother had been in touch with him, and that she wanted to see me. 'She's rung the flat a few times,' he said nervously. 'The last time she called she said that your father's had a heart attack.'

Despite everything that had happened between my father and I, my heart sank when Oliver told me that he was ill. Caring was, and still is, a huge part of my character and I've always continued to care about people, even if they've mistreated me. By caring and opening myself up to people, I had allowed myself to get hurt – but I realised now that caring didn't necessarily mean being a victim. One thing I have learned is that the power of forgiveness is the greatest gift of all.

After Oliver's call, I knew one thing: I was still very much afraid of my mother. I feared calling her, I feared seeing her face and I wasn't sure I was ready to do either. I also knew that I'd have to tell the police that she'd tried to make contact and then decide what to do.

The police told me I could call her and meet her if I really wanted to and that they would watch us from afar. I would need to keep my phone switched on and to meet her in a public place. They stressed that, if my father was sick, it was important for me to do what I needed to. I felt better knowing that they'd given me the all-clear. It was up to me to take the next step.

It was exactly four months since the text from Saira when I finally plucked up the courage and made the call home. I was nervous when I first heard my mother's voice on the phone, but I tried to sound strong.

'It's me, Mum. It's Sofia,' I said calmly.

'I won't harm you, Sofia. I just want to talk. I'm worried

that your father is going to die and I also want to explain myself,' my mother replied breathlessly. 'Can we meet in Brighton tonight?'

I felt my heart beat faster. It was all happening so quickly. But, like her, I didn't want to waste any more time. There was nothing else for me to say until my mother had explained herself. We agreed a meeting place in Brighton and hung up.

I took a deep breath and decided to focus hard on the meeting. My instincts told me that my mother was telling the truth and that she wanted to make peace with me. I trusted her about that. Strange as it may seem, I also felt that, eventually, I might even be able to forgive her.

That night, we met on a busy street in Brighton, the police looking on from afar. It was about 8.30pm when I spotted my mother standing in the shadows by her car. I walked towards her and pulled my winter coat tight around my body.

'Hi, Mum,' I said. I felt stronger than I thought I would as I faced her in the darkness, and at the same time I was pricked by a confusing mixture of love and pain. 'Let's go for a walk down to the seafront,' I said. It felt good being in control for once, and it really mattered to me that she realised that I was.

My mother bowed her head and we walked in silence, side by side, along one of the dimly lit cobbled lanes towards the seafront. I walked slowly so that the police could follow us until we stopped by the pier and faced the sea.

The sea looked just the same as it had all those years ago. It had given me such strength back then, and it was doing the same now. I felt thankful as I watched it in all its glory in front of me. I listened to the waves crashing against the shore and watched the frothing water swirling freely around the shingle on the beach.

'How's Dad?' I asked, breaking the silence.

'He's getting better today, it seems. I was worried about him and I thought you should know.' She paused. 'But I didn't really come about your father, Sofia. I wanted to explain myself.'

'I know. I just wanted to know that Dad was OK and then listen to what you've got to say.'

I looked at her expectantly.

'I was told that you were working as a prostitute,' she began. 'I needed to either get you home or forget you. I was told this and so thought you were dishonouring your family. Being a prostitute is the worst dishonour I could ever imagine my daughter to have bestowed upon my family. You've always known full well that we need to maintain our honour at whatever cost. Even at the cost of our own lives.'

She had spoken coldly, but her voice softened as she continued.

'I had no choice. But I won't hurt you now. You're a stronger woman than I ever could be, Sofia, because you've broken free,' she said sadly. 'Sometimes I wish I had the strength that you have.'

I couldn't reply. At first I felt confused but I also felt angry. I wasn't a prostitute and I didn't know why, or how, my mother had thought I was. I understood about my family's honour and how much it meant to them. I knew that my mother knew no different and that, accordingly, she was a very weak woman. But I still had the right to be free and her words had angered me.

'When you ran away, a man kept phoning our house and speaking to everyone in the family,' she continued. 'He told us where you were and what you were doing. He said you were working the streets of Brighton. He gave me his address and his number and he told me you lived close by so I sent one of the family to you. I told him I would come and see him afterwards. I couldn't have my child working as a prostitute, Sofia. We tried to tell you before, but you didn't listen and ran away, so I took a bigger step to stop you working as a prostitute.

'He told me that he'd contacted me because he thought you were in danger wandering the streets at night, but he didn't want you to know that he'd called. If you ever came into the room when he was on the phone, he'd hang up. I heard your voice once and I assumed that this man was telling the truth.'

As I listened to everything that my mother said, all became clear. I realised exactly what had happened. Maybe Omar *had* been afraid or he'd been trying to get revenge. But, whatever the reason behind his deceitful actions, I wasn't a prostitute and felt terribly betrayed and sick that he'd told my mother that I was. My misgivings about Omar being the person who told my mother I was a prostitute may have been incorrect, but it all seemed to point to that – and I couldn't think of anyone else it could have been.

My anger with my mother began to subside.

'It's OK, Mum,' I said. 'I'm not a prostitute. I'm a hard-working, decent young woman with dreams and a lot of love to give. I'm doing really well now. I'm fine. I just want to be able to get on with my life like I deserve to. I'm not hurting anyone or doing any harm. You need to let me live life my own way now.'

Confusion and anger left me. Whatever she had done, my mother had at least found the courage to come to talk to me and accept her weakness. She didn't say sorry for kidnapping me or for thinking about killing me, but I knew that deep down she *was* sorry, and for that I couldn't be angry with her any longer. In her own way, I know that my mother was trying to make peace. She also admitted that my father wasn't as ill as she had made out – she had embellished the truth so that she could speak to me.

There was an outstanding problem, though. My mother still wanted me to give up my dream of performing. Unable to look me in the eye, she told me she still wanted me to be a good Muslim girl.

'But God has given me this passion and talent, Mum. I can't be happy without it so I need to follow my dream. I'm free and I am going to perform, family or no family. It's you who needs to change.'

She pleaded with me to give it up, to keep performing as a hobby.

'No,' I replied. 'I can't give it up, it's part of who I am. You said that God makes everything happen, why didn't he make me want to be a doctor or a lawyer? Why did he give me this passion and ambition to perform? Why would he do that, Mum?'

'Then you need to make a choice, Sofia. You need to choose between your performance and us. We've made peace now and I won't harm you or try to bring you back home again, but I still want you to be a decent woman who isn't in this performance world.'

'Why can't I have both, Mum? I need my mother and I need the freedom to perform.'

'It's your family, or your performing, Sofia.'

'Then you make the choice, Mum, because I want both. Taking away performing would be taking away "Sofia" and her freedom. I've come too far to go back. Freedom is no use to me without being able to perform. You talked about strength tonight, and I am stronger because of this.'

It was then that Mum snapped. 'I will tell everyone I don't have a fourth daughter any more. I've lost you. I have no choice. You are dead in my eyes.'

She walked briskly off into the night. My mother had vanished. I closed my eyes, but I couldn't cry. I knew that it wasn't my mother saying those words – it was honour and her false belief in it that gave her no choice. I lost my mother that night, and I would not get her back for many years. It was so tough, but the upside was that I stopped fearing her because I'd stuck my ground. I could have given up my dreams that night and gone back home with her, but my dreams were much stronger than anything else and I was slowly becoming the person I was meant to be.

To this day, I don't fear my mother and I don't feel angry with her. I have forgiven her, but I do carry a huge amount of sadness about the death threat that my mother placed on me. The memories of that sad, lonely and fearful time will probably never fade completely.

CHAPTER TWELVE

SURGERY

A huge weight had been lifted from my shoulders. Because my mother had cut me off, I could wholeheartedly change my life and fully embrace my freedom. When I finished my degree, I would be able to pursue performing as a career. But I had a more pressing matter to attend to first. I wanted to get a nose job.

Having a pretty new nose would help me say goodbye to the bullies from my past. I felt that over time I could perhaps forgive them, as I'd forgiven my mother, but to do so I needed to do something concrete. I wanted to prevent people from harming me further. I needed to say 'hello' to a new Sofia to make a fresh new start.

I'd always been very conscious of my big, hooked nose – whenever I went out I'd wear my hair down so it was as concealed as possible. I couldn't forget the jibes and taunts from the past. I'd look at my nose in the mirror every day, and it still made me feel vulnerable. On a deeper, more psychological level, because my nose had taken on the exact shape as my father's and my uncle's had, it only reminded me of everything that I'd been through as a child. The appearance my nose gave me seemed to connect me with these two men, and I needed to try to sever that connection.

I'd known I wanted to change my nose before my mother had left me on the pier that night, but it wasn't until I made that final break with her that I had the space in my mind to go further. One day, soon after the pier incident, I was walking along the road in Brighton when I realised I was ready to start looking into surgery properly.

That day, some kids had whistled at me because I was wearing a short skirt. 'Hey, gorgeous!' one of them had shouted over at me. I wasn't facing them, so I knew that they were complimenting me on my legs and figure, but not my face. For a moment or two it felt good that these youngsters had said that I was gorgeous, so I carried on walking down the road confidently.

But as I walked on I started to challenge myself, and the compliment. Deep down, I knew that the boys would make a nasty remark about my nose if I turned around. In the past, I wouldn't have had the courage to turn and face them, but during that time I'd begun to challenge myself a bit in order to become stronger. I bravely turned around and walked back into their view.

'Oh, look at her ugly big nose!' they shouted predictably, and laughed with one another.

It was hard, but because I'd got the reaction that I'd expected I knew that I needed to make the change. I didn't want to be a girl who walked down the street and couldn't turn her head to smile at the boys who were whistling at her. I wanted to be the girl who could walk down the street with her head held high and turn happily to face her admirers.

I'd never even smiled in a photo or in front of men, because smiling made my nose look wider. When I look at photos from my past, I can't help but feel sad. There is one school photo of me where I am smiling and, because my eyes and nose were growing faster than everything else, they looked huge.

I looked into surgery and to my horror found that a decent nose job would set me back at least £4000. I was busy studying and didn't have that kind of money, so I waited and had the operation a year or so later. In the meantime I simply read up about it in various magazines and watched several TV programmes about it. I knew that the operation would be painful and that people got black eyes and had to be wrapped up in bandages for two weeks, but those things didn't deter me. All I cared about was the emotional pain that my big nose was causing me, and how insecure it always made me feel.

At the end of my university course, my friend Paul told me that he knew of a good cosmetic surgeon up in Liverpool and that he'd help fund the operation. He knew how important it was to me, and really wanted to help. He had listened when I told him about all the sniggering boys in the street and the bullying that I'd endured as a child, and was so kind about it all. He told me that the surgeon he knew would be able to give me whatever I wanted. I was so grateful to him for his kindness.

'Let's book it!' I said, hugging him. 'I'll pay you back, though, I promise!'

Paul was fantastic, and organised everything for me. He

took the money I had left over from my student grant to pay the deposit, and then used some of his savings to make up the £4500 I needed.

It was perfect timing. I had just finished my degree course and desperately wanted to start my performing career. A new nose would be a brand-new start for me.

The next day I booked a bus ticket and got ready to travel for three hours to meet the surgeon in Liverpool. I was really anxious as Paul and I waited for the bus to arrive – although the decision had been made, it was all happening so quickly and I hadn't had much time to think. I would be operated on that day and back in Brighton by the weekend. It was all happening so quickly, but my experience told me that 'quick' is often the best way.

'You'll be fine, Sofia. I can't wait to see the new you!' Paul said as we hugged at the bus station.

I climbed on to the bus. I was on my way.

I was still very nervous when I arrived at the surgeon's office, mainly because I was alone. I didn't know the man who was going to break my nose, or anything about the surgery, but the surgeon noticed my fear and calmly talked me through everything. There would be bruising, pain and bandaging, but I would be well looked after and painkillers would keep things under control.

'This is an exciting time!' he said as he took Polaroids of my face and its uneven profile.

I'd brought up a picture of the nose that I thought would look perfect on my face. I'd cut it out of American *Playboy* and, when I'd spotted it, I really thought it was the perfect nose!

The next thing I knew I was lying on the operating

122

table. The surgeon smiled down at me warmly. 'Just relax, Sofia. I'll see you in a bit,' he said, and that was it.

When I woke up, I was in so much pain. I couldn't move until the nurse came in and helped me sit upright so that I could wake up a bit. I remember desperately needing the bathroom and her helping me walk to the toilet. The nurse told me to have a quick look in the mirror. I couldn't wait to see what my nose looked like, but when I stared in the mirror my face looked like a car crash. I felt complete horror.

'I wish that I hadn't done this now!' I cried at the nurse as I tried to touch my face. There was a thick white plaster stuck straight across my cheeks and nose and there was swelling and bruising everywhere. It wasn't just confined to my eyes – it travelled right across to my ears. But the worst thing was the pain. It seared through my skull and all the way down my back. It was the most unbearable agony I'd ever felt.

'We need to dose you up with a lot of painkillers,' said the nurse. 'After an hour you'll feel better. The painkillers will get you through the day and night.' She handed me two large white pills and a glass of water.

I felt better after that, but I was still quite upset by what I'd seen in the mirror.

An hour later, the surgeon came in and removed the bandages. He knew that I was upset because I couldn't even speak. The bandages were completely soaked in blood. Then, to make matters worse, blood started to pour out of my nose as the surgeon pulled out the final bits of gauze that had been packed tightly inside my nostrils. I can only describe the feeling as like having my brain sucked out. I could see steam coming from the blood as it poured from my nose. It gushed out into the bowl the nurse was holding, and I passed out!

I don't remember much after that apart from sitting alone on the bus back to Brighton with a baseball cap pulled over my eyes and a pink plaster strip stretched across my swollen, blackened face. I didn't care that I must've looked strange, because I just wanted to get home and into bed. I remember feeling weak and disorientated as I tried to sleep in the back seat. I couldn't wait to see Paul's friendly face at the bus depot.

The next week, I turned up at university to get my degree results with a plaster on my nose. I remember rolling up and everyone shrieking at me because they thought I'd been in an accident. I remember a few of my course mates were sitting on a bench in the courtyard and they couldn't believe what I looked like.

'Oh, I've just had surgery,' I said, smiling. It sounded so grown up. I couldn't and didn't want to lie.

Seeing how happy I was, my friends hugged me tightly. What they didn't know was that I'd just erased the last connection with my horrible, painful past and that the bullying I'd suffered would never happen again.

No one knew what I'd been through as a school kid, or about my uncle and father. No one knew about the laundry factory. No one knew what I'd been through at home in Kent. But none of it mattered at that moment. I was just so thrilled because my friends were admiring and accepting the brand-new me with open arms.

'It's great, Sofia!' they all said. 'You'll look amazing!'

I couldn't have felt happier and more loved.

Two weeks passed. I was due back at the surgery, but I couldn't handle the trip back to Liverpool, so I took the stitches out myself! It was really painful but I did it very carefully with antiseptic wipes. The local doctor in Brighton took the plaster off. My face still looked like a football and my eyes were still both sunken and black. My nose was also really dirty because it hadn't been cleaned for two weeks. But the main thing was that it looked so pretty and straight. I was overjoyed with my new nose. I didn't care about the swelling or the money because I knew that my life would be heaps better and that I'd done the right thing.

It took two years to see the full effect of my nose job; the initial swelling goes down after three weeks, but it takes two years for the nose to shrink to the size it's supposed to be. After three weeks, however, the bruising had practically gone and I covered any remaining traces of it with make-up.

After my nose job, people said that I smiled and interacted with them a lot more. I felt so much happier with my face. I didn't feel the need to wear as much make-up and felt confident wearing my hair tied back. I bought hundreds of pretty hair slides and colourful hair bands and experimented with my hair for the first time ever.

And I never heard another remark made about my nose.

Finally, I had extinguished the old me. I didn't dwell on the bullies or the racist remarks any more and I didn't think about my father and uncle when I stared in the mirror each day. All I saw was a refined nose and a much happier, more feminine face.

I was ready for the life I wanted. I was ready to get into acting and singing as soon as possible. With my family at a distance and my pretty new nose in place, I'd well and truly managed to step away from my past and was looking forward to a bright and happy future.

I was ready to perform.

CHAPTER THIRTEEN
STARTING OUT

In 1998, I graduated with a third. It wasn't the best of grades, but, considering what I'd been through in my personal life, I was really pleased that I'd actually managed to pass. I also felt excited when I left university. I was 24 and I had a whole new life ahead of me. I couldn't wait to get my first taste of the real world of performing.

The first performance-type thing that I wanted to do after graduating was to set up a girl band. I'd met two girls at the beginning of my degree course and thought we'd make a good act, but because of the Michael Jackson incident and the subsequent backlash from my parents, I'd never had the courage to approach the girls about my idea, let alone to get up on stage and perform.

After my finals, I felt ready to chat to the girls – Shanila and Jessica – about my idea. Shanila had become a friend and confidante after Peter had left me and was warm, sexy and genuine. She was from Mauritius and had a strong and beautiful exotic look about her. Jessica was a dancer and single mother so she was very headstrong and capable. We'd been sitting having coffee in a café when I blurted it out, praying that they wouldn't laugh.

'Let's start a band!' I said, sipping my cappuccino. 'We'd make a perfect trio. We all look good and we can all sing.'

They hadn't laughed yet, so I continued.

'We can gig around Brighton and start to make a name for ourselves. What do you think?'

They loved the idea, and seemed just as excited as I was, so we hatched a plan together. We chatted about what we wanted to sing and how we wanted to look, and then we thought up a name. We all looked down at the bowl of brown sugar on the table and it just came to us: Sugar Brown. It sounded perfect – we were all dark skinned and thought we had sweet, mouth-watering looks.

I wanted to get everything under way as quickly as possible, so that afternoon I sat down and devised a strategy. I knew that we needed to record and produce a couple of decent tracks together, but first of all we really needed to get some decent photos taken. I called a photographer I knew from the Brighton clubbing scene and she kindly offered to do a shoot for us at a minimal cost.

With the photoshoot coming up, it was time to hit the shops to sort out our styling. We all loved the same type of clothes, and ended up with three cheap and cheerful outfits in different shades of brown and gold from Miss Selfridge.

A few weeks later, it felt like our dreams were starting to come true as we posed happily in the studio wearing our tiny skirts and sultry tops. It was my first ever shoot, and, though we were all novices, our shots ended up looking really great.

The next step was to try to record some of the songs

we'd already started to write. We had met up a few times and sat through the night in my bedroom singing harmonies using lyrics that I'd written. We loved the sound and we really had high hopes.

Once the songs began to take shape, and with our photos done, we tried to get ourselves into a studio to produce our tracks professionally. It all sounded so easy, but the difficulty was that we didn't have any money between us. We were lucky with the photographer, but we weren't so fortunate when it came to looking for free, or cut-price, rehearsal space and a studio producer.

We spent a week calling everyone we knew in Brighton, but no one had any spare cash or any time to help us out. Eventually, I suggested that we all needed to save up and just hang on to what we had in the meantime. We could keep practising and try again when we had more money in our pockets.

'Let's not lose hope,' I said to the girls.

But Shanila and Jessica didn't want to wait, and unfortunately they both gave up on me.

I was so disappointed that the girls had given up so quickly and easily. But looking back, *not* giving up was exactly why I was the one who got somewhere in the end. Shanila and Jessica vanished from my life, which was a shame. The saddest thing was that those two had such great talent, yet they didn't seem to have the drive to nourish it. I had the passion and the determination and I knew that I had talent. It was a necessary combination that carried me through the start of my career and is still carrying me through it today. I did meet Shanila again, through Facebook. She has set up her own nightclub in Brighton and seems really happy.

I wasn't really prepared for what lay ahead. Looking back, I can see that I had so much to learn. A long hard road was ahead of me. Being talented, determined and passionate was a great starting point; being young, inexperienced and like a million other aspiring performers wasn't so great at all.

I began looking for acting or singing work while still shifting every day at Legal & General. My first port of call was finding a decent research tool, and *The Stage* – a newspaper containing all sorts of adverts and listings for acting and singing jobs, castings and band auditions – soon became my bible.

I sat on my bed every Thursday morning and trawled through it religiously. Then I set to work calling up anyone and everyone who I thought might be interested in seeing me. If they were interested, I would take the day off work and head up to London. I stuck to my strict routine during this time, and after a few months I was traipsing up to London at least once a week to audition. My work were fine with me taking the time out as I was working shifts and always made up my hours.

It was such an exciting time – everything was new to me and I met so many great people. At the same time, it was quite tough because there were so many rejections to cope with. My first ever casting was in London for a new teen band. That day, I assumed everyone would be dressed casually or in dance gear, so I put on a pair of black combat trousers, a fitted T-shirt and trainers with a matching cap and travelled up to Pineapple Dance Studios in Covent Garden.

I didn't know what on earth to expect, but when I arrived I was completely overwhelmed by the vast number of girls auditioning for the same band. What's more, I ended up queuing for three hours!

'They've already decided who they want,' said one of the girls who was standing confidently in front of me, flicking her perfectly styled blonde hair. 'It's not worth getting your hopes up with this one.'

'What do you mean? They're auditioning, aren't they?' I said. I was already really nervous, but after chatting to the girl I felt really despondent.

She explained that the producers already had an idea of who they actually wanted and she thought they were just going through the motions with everyone else who was in the queue.

When my name was finally called, I knew that it was highly unlikely that I'd be called back, but I decided to do what I could anyway. I held my head up high, went into the audition room and stood calmly in front of the panel of four judges. I looked around, unsure what was going to happen next. All I could see was the judges' faces, wall-to-wall mirrors and a huge stereo system standing in the corner on the floor.

'Sofia Hayat. You may start,' said one of the male judges, without looking up from his notepad. I noticed that a female judge was saying something under her breath.

Trying not to care, I opened my mouth and began to sing. Although I was confident in my voice, the situation was new to me so I was nervous as I sang 'Killing Me Softly'.

'Stop! That's enough,' yelled the whispering women after a few moments. She had bright-yellow hair, black horn-rimmed glasses and thick red lips. 'You've an excellent voice and look, Miss Hayat, but you obviously haven't done your homework. You haven't even checked the brief properly, have you?'

Without waiting for an answer, she whispered something else to the woman sitting next to her. They then both looked up and smirked. It was really like something out of *X Factor*. I knew there and then that I'd failed, but I also realised that I'd learned something. It was true that I hadn't asked for a brief when I'd called up about the audition, but then I didn't even know what a brief was! I hadn't prepared myself for that first audition because I really didn't know how.

Although I was upset because of the rejection, looking back now I can just laugh at it. I do wish that I'd been more prepared back then, but remembering those early mistakes only makes me realise how far I've actually come. After that first catastrophe I travelled back home to Brighton, set my heart on the next audition and consoled myself with the knowledge that I'd learned something. It was still just the beginning, I told myself.

The following week, I went back up to Pineapple Studios to audition for another band. This time I wanted to look a bit sexier so I wore a pair of blue jeans, a trendy white T-shirt and heels. I gasped when I turned the corner from Long Acre on to Langley Street – the queue was even longer than last time. It stretched all the way up the road. I took a deep breath and wandered down to the end of the line. I waited patiently for about an hour or so until the judging panel appeared on the steps outside the studio.

I watched them walking down the queue choosing what they must have considered to be the best-looking kids. They then sent all the others home. I wasn't chosen, which was obviously frustrating, but I was more annoyed at having taken the day off work for nothing. But I carried on and just made sure that I learned from each experience as I travelled through the new and exciting world of showbiz.

At some of the auditions I had to dance before I sang to the judges. I particularly enjoyed doing those ones, but the problem I had was that, while my degree was in Performing Arts, my course had been drama based so I wasn't a trained dancer. It took longer for me to perfect the moves and often the other girls and choreographers grew fed up with me lagging behind. The first time that this happened I felt so embarrassed at my lack of skill that I left the studio before my name was called.

Those times were quite hard for me emotionally. I'd learned how to dance from the stage at The Paradox and from watching TV, plus I knew that I was a natural, but most of the other kids that I was auditioning with were Italia Conti or Webber Douglas students. Unlike them, I'd never had enough money to take proper dance classes or buy colourful, trendy dance outfits.

At some auditions, I got upset about my parents and my past. I'd often look around the audition halls and notice that most of the other kids had their mothers or fathers (and sometimes both parents) alongside them. Parents would stand patiently with their kids in the queue and then wait for them, their hands clasped together in anticipation, outside the audition rooms. They seemed to give their children such fantastic moral support and I'd get quite envious whenever I saw them hugging and kissing their children when their audition had finished.

My heart often sank because it was so different for me. My parents had no idea who or where I was any more. They had no idea I was attending singing or acting auditions up in London, and no idea that I was all made up and looking pretty. All I knew was that they would've been distraught if they'd seen me standing there looking like that. They would have been so angry and upset that I was finally performing. I always had to try to blot those thoughts from my mind – if I didn't I knew that I wouldn't audition well.

It was difficult not to feel alone and upset during those moments, but after a few minutes my loneliness just made me want to fight harder. I didn't have trendy dance outfits or the right training, money in my pocket or support from a father and mother who loved me. But what I did have was the freedom to nurture my talent. I also had the eternal will to relentlessly following my dream.

A few months in, I got lucky. I was selected for a new band called The Word On The Street. The audition was at Pineapple Studios again, and as usual the place was heaving with hundreds of exuberant youngsters just like me. I stood happily in the long queue and listened to some of the other kids in front of me chat about another huge project that was in audition on the floor upstairs.

'They want under-18s and are looking at prospective singers and dancers in our queue!' said a pretty redhead.

Just as I was about to ask her what she meant, a man came up to me and asked me to go upstairs to the audition.

'But I'm 24,' I told him.

'Oh it's fine,' he said. 'I really like your look. We want a dark, exotic singer and you look perfect.'

He smiled as he ushered me to the front of the queue and showed me to the entrance door. I held my head up high and walked past the pretty redhead, who was whispering that I was too old to the other kids in the queue. Not that

I cared – my heart was bursting with excitement as I followed the man up the stairs to an audition room.

I auditioned and won the part. I was over the moon.

'We really like you, Sofia,' said the producer. 'Do you have an agent we can chat to?'

'No, not yet,' I replied, unsure if I was saying the right thing. 'But I want to get one. I'm new to all of this...'

'OK, well, we'll be in touch. The band is called S Club 7 and we have high hopes.'

I gave them my details and went back downstairs.

I had no idea what to do. My name was still down on the list for the other audition and I wasn't sure if I should go for it. In the end I decided to take a chance and go ahead with that one too. I auditioned and got that part too!

'This band has already got a manager in place, Miss Hayat, and the songs are already ready. We want to start next month. Are you free?' they said to me after I'd sung my heart out.

I made my mind up on the spot.

'Yes. Count me in!'

I was totally thrilled. I'd declined S Club 7, but I was a member of The Word On The Street and I was on cloud nine. Little did I know then how big S Club 7 would go on to become! I got back home, called Legal & General and everyone congratulated me and wished me luck. I couldn't wait to start work on the band.

There were five of us – three girls and two boys. We moved into a house in North London and started work straight away. I was really happy just being involved in the project, even though I wasn't that taken with the tracks that they wanted us to sing.

The band was produced by Ian Levine, who was highly

respected at the time because of his successful work with Take That. Although I'd never met Ian before, he'd seen the audition tapes and told our management team that he really liked my look and voice. I was very keen to work with him, but, when we eventually met, the attention Ian gave me started to cause problems among the other girls in the band.

I was often asked to show the others how to sing because Ian liked the way I used my voice. I didn't mind at first because I was slightly older than the other girls, but after a few days it was obvious they couldn't stand being shown anything by me. I soon began to feel left out.

By the time it all became too much for me, we'd already recorded a few songs and were in the throes of starting our initial publicity rounds.

'You remind me of Dina Carroll,' Ian said one day as the others stood next to me. 'You could be a solo star.'

I blushed. I was pleased that Ian saw something in me, but it made things a bit more difficult between the other girls and me.

Things were becoming really tough. And they only got worse.

On our first photoshoot, what should have been an exciting day for me turned into a bit of a nightmare. Ian had placed me in the middle of the group, but the girls weren't particularly happy about that.

In the end, there just wasn't the chemistry between me and the other girls, so I left.

All in all, my first year in the performing world was pretty tough. It seemed to me that the music industry was very competitive, bitchy and hard to break into. There were so many auditions going on, and so many young stars out there, that sometimes I didn't feel like I'd ever get anywhere. Even being selected was never a promise of real success.

The Word On The Street didn't make it to the top. I didn't care because I knew that I had to keep persevering and that one day I would need to do so alone, as a solo artist. The more auditions I went to and the harder I tried, the more I learned and improved. I always reminded myself to take the knocks with a pinch of salt and to take things slowly.

It was at this time that I started to date again. I had met a man who I will call Stuart, who was tall and handsome with gorgeous green eyes and a great body. He was well spoken and had what I thought was a kindness in his eyes. I was happy at first – he supported me and gave me a hug when I needed one. Plus, he was very loving and sensual. Sadly, I then started to witness some aggression in Stuart. He would shout, and, once, on a night out, he even threw me against a car. I knew that I'd had enough aggression in my life and was a stronger person than I had been when I was at university – so I left him.

After spending a year trying to get a music break, I decided I needed to make further changes to my lifestyle in order to pick up the pace. I was apart from my family and I'd put my love life on hold, but I wasn't happy being strapped for cash all the time. I couldn't afford singing and acting lessons, proper audition outfits or time in recording studios, so I decided to start earning decent money.

It was time to leave Brighton for London. I knew that I could earn much more up there, and that I'd save on all the travelling. I also assumed being in London would enable me to make more industry contacts.

I put my CV on the internet in 2000, and to my surprise a new, City-based recruitment company contacted me straight away. I was also astounded by the pay they were offering – they signed me up on £30,000 basic, plus commission. I'd never thought I would be able to earn anything like that. I started the job straight away and was soon raking in around £4000 a month. I was beginning to really flourish. I had a good social life with the girls at work, and the agency were great about giving me time off for auditions. And it felt fantastic having so much money in my account.

After I'd settled in at work, I began flat hunting in London. I decided to look for a small flat around Fulham and Chelsea – they seemed safe and classy areas – and after a few weeks I settled on a small one-bedroom flat on Edith Grove. The flat was well decorated and clean and had a private balcony overlooking a pretty little garden. I felt great – I finally had my own home! Joaquin had been great to live with in Brighton, but until then I'd been constantly living under someone else's feet. Being fully independent made me feel totally self-sufficient.

The night before the move, I collected a van from a local hire company in Brighton and packed everything up, ready for the next day. I went to bed early so that I was refreshed and energised for the next morning. I'd taken two days off work just so that I could do everything quickly and efficiently on my own.

The spring sunshine woke me up early on my last day in Brighton. It was literally bursting its way through my bedroom window as if to tell me to get up and enjoy the day. I jumped out of bed and dressed quickly. I couldn't wait to get out of the bedroom and make a new start in my first ever home.

I left Joaquin a farewell card with my new address in it, climbed into the van and sped off in the bright morning sunshine. I was really tired from all the packing and carrying, but at the same time exhilarated and excited thinking about what lay ahead in London.

As I looked for the sign for the motorway I thought about all the house moves I'd made since I'd left my family home on Northcote Road. It had been frustrating and painful at times, especially when I'd run away and had had nowhere to go, but I'd always somehow managed to find the strength to pull through.

As I drove past Brighton pier I thought of my parents, who would just be waking up in their house. I remembered my wooden bunk bed and the mattress I'd slept on in the cellar. I wondered if my parents ever thought about me and what I was up to. I wondered if my mother knew that I was safe and doing well, and if she even missed me. I didn't really miss her much by then because my life was clearly on an upward spiral.

I was happy following my dreams and thoroughly enjoying being on my own. I was so much stronger than before. Slowly but surely, I'd found my feet. I was able to rely on myself and did not need the support or approval of a family.

I looked in the wing mirror and watched Brighton pier disappear behind me. I felt sad because Brighton had been the place I'd first discovered and tasted a small sense of freedom. Brighton had inspired, challenged and changed me, and I knew that one day I might even return. Even though I felt sad when the pier eventually disappeared out of my sight, I knew that the sea was still something that symbolised so much for me. It represented power and freedom, just as it had done all those years ago when I stood before it for the first time. I felt hopeful about my future as I put my foot down on the accelerator.

As I settled into my new routine in London, I started to thrive. I got up early every morning, ate my breakfast on my balcony, and watched the birds in the trees in the garden below. The garden often reminded me of the one at Northcote Road, where the train would chuff past me and I'd want to escape into the countryside. I felt so much happier than I'd done back then.

After breakfast I'd take the tube to Bishopsgate, work at the recruitment agency, and then spend the evenings at work events or in the recording studio. I was finally able to really enjoy a decent and prosperous lifestyle while pursuing my performing dream.

I had no urge to run away any more. The balance I'd finally struck was perfect.

CHAPTER FOURTEEN

LONDON AND LEONARDO

Just after I arrived in London, I was selected for a new three-piece girl band. I had found out about the audition in *The Stage*, turned up at a small studio in Covent Garden and sung my heart out in front of three producers. I felt particularly happy that day, and it must have shown – they offered me the job on the spot! I was thrilled because I loved what the band was all about. It had Asian influences and our manager was a man who was already a respected producer and composer, Biddu. Among his production credits was the hit 'Kung Fu Fighting', but we were the first band he managed.

There were three of us in the band: me, Jyoti and Jas. I remember that the other two were thinner than me, a fact that the management were always pointing out. We all set to work, recorded about four songs and were eager to get ourselves signed. The only downside was that I was eventually told to lose weight! I was about 11 stone at that stage so I was put on a strict diet where they weighed me every day and told me what to eat. I found it all a bit tiresome – I was happy with my figure! – but I knew that I had to do as they said. After I'd lost a bit of the weight I decided to take things further and change my whole look.

I'd never experimented with different hair colours before, but I dyed my hair a pretty honey colour and ended up looking like Jennifer Lopez! I was over the moon with my new hair colour, but unfortunately the other girls didn't like it one bit.

They didn't think that J-Lo was the right look for the band and suggested that I dye my hair a different colour.

'I can't do that, Jas,' I replied. 'This is *me*. You're trying to pigeonhole me. This isn't how I like to work and I can't thrive like this as an artist. You sound like my mother used to sound.'

In the end, I decided to leave the band. After my stint with Biddu failed, I tried my hand at going solo. There had been far too many problems when I'd worked with other girls. Also, going solo would be a bigger challenge for me, and a bigger challenge was just what I wanted.

It was the winter of 2001 when I set to work on my vocals. I began paying for more singing lessons and auditioned tirelessly for months. It took a while but eventually a music manager called Tyrese picked up on me. At the time Tyrese was looking after a successful female three-piece called Cleopatra, and when he spotted me at an audition he offered to take me on. Naturally, I was thrilled, and we started recording tracks with his producer while Tyrese went out looking for a music deal.

Unbeknown to me, Tyrese was friends with a man who looked after high-profile celebrities whenever they flew into London. I only found out about this one night after we'd finished work at the studio.

'My friend's client is coming into town for his film premiere tomorrow night,' Tyrese said.

'Which client of your friend?' I asked nonchalantly as I put my coat on. I was cold and tired after a long day and all I wanted to do was to climb into my warm, cosy bed.

'Leonardo DiCaprio. My friend takes care of him. He's asked me to come along with some friends for some pre-premiere-night drinks in town. You should come.'

'Oh right,' I said, completely unsure of what to do or say. 'Um, what time?

'Nine o'clock. It's at 57 Jermyn Street,' said Tyrese as he disappeared out of the door.

I had never been particularly interested in the celebrity world and wasn't especially bothered about spending time with Leonardo DiCaprio, but at the same time I knew that it might be a good opportunity for me to make some decent acting contacts.

I'd go and meet Leonardo, but I had to get ready first.

I went home, ran a deep bubble bath and soaked my body in the hot soapy water. My body was aching because of the long hours that I was doing at the recruitment company combined with working late into the night at the recording studio. I was so tired.

The next thing I knew, my mobile was ringing in the living room.

'Sofia, where are you? It's 9.30!' barked Tyrese.

I'd drifted off to sleep in the bath!

'Oh, I'm almost ready. Sorry, Tyrese,' I stuttered, trying to stop the soapy water dripping off me and soaking my living-room carpet.

'Hurry up then, because we're all here,' he said, and hung up.

I rushed back into the bathroom, grabbed a towel and dried myself off. I threw on a pair of smart Gucci trousers and a fitted deep-red Versace top, combed my hair through and applied some deep-red glossy lipstick. I remember looking in the hallway mirror before leaving the flat and thinking how good I'd started to feel, despite all the work I was doing. It's because I'm so much happier, I thought.

I got in a cab, began to wake up properly and started to feel excited about the evening ahead. As we approached the heart of the West End, I felt glad that Tyrese had been so pushy with me about coming out. I watched the crowds of people milling along Piccadilly in the cold, glittering night and drew a deep breath – I was so enamoured by it all.

People crowded around the underground stations either heading home from drinks after work or heading out for a night of West End fun. As the bright lights of Piccadilly Circus captivated me, I realised that I'd been missing out a little. I needed to start injecting a bit more excitement into my life again.

The cab turned a corner and stopped outside a small, dimly lit entrance on Jermyn Street. 'This is 57. You need to go down the stairs to the basement,' the cabbie said as I paid him and got out.

I found my way down a black metal stairwell and pushed open a big black door. I dropped off my coat and entered the room. Number 57 had an amazingly intimate feel to it, and the bar was small and chic. I soon spotted a happy-looking Leo hanging out with his friends at a table in the back section. Tyrese and a few of his music friends were sipping cocktails on the next table so I went over and joined them.

'Hey, how are you all? Sorry I'm so late. I had to relax for a bit,' I explained.

'No problem, Sofia, I'm just glad you made it. Have a drink with us and I'll introduce you to everyone,' Tyrese said, smiling and taking my hand. 'You look amazing,' he added as we made our way around the VIP section.

I noticed straight away that there weren't many girls there, but it didn't unnerve me and I just got stuck into the party. I still hadn't thought about meeting Leo at all, because that night I'd pinned my hopes on making some good contacts.

After an hour of chatting to Tyrese and his friends, Tyrese introduced me to Leo. 'This is one of my brightest new stars, Sofia Hayat,' he said, smiling at Leo, and then at me. 'Isn't she stunning, Leo?'

Leo nodded and smiled, but all I did was blush. It was flattering to hear Tyrese say that to another man and for another man to agree with him. Before I could say anything Leo kissed me on both cheeks. I blushed again – although I hadn't wanted to be, I was left speechless.

I was suddenly so nervous and flustered in front of this seemingly handsome man, and I hadn't anticipated feeling like that at all. I say 'seemingly' because I couldn't see Leo's face properly. The bar was so dimly lit and he was wearing a baseball cap, but I could see he was charming.

'Do you want a vodka tonic with me, Sofia?' said Leo quietly.

'Sure,' I replied, my stomach fluttering.

Leo ushered me over to a seat at his table where we sat and chatted together for the next few hours. We didn't really talk about anything important, just how bad the English weather was and how I was working on a new recording project. I remember thinking how sweet and angelic Leo looked, like a little boy. He was so generous to everyone, constantly pouring us drinks. When the bill came, Leo questioned it, which made me laugh – he obviously hadn't realised how much we'd all been drinking!

'Will you come back to the hotel with us, Sofia?' Leo asked me as the waitress wandered off with his card.

Everyone else was excited and had already started to filter out of the bar, but my tiredness had started to kick in again, and I felt lost for words.

On the one hand, I'd planned to head home, but on the other we were having such a great time that part of me wanted to go with them all.

'Um, it's 2am. I'm not sure,' I said, looking at my watch. 'I've got to work tomorrow and I'm pretty exhausted.'

'Oh come on,' encouraged Leo. 'You only live once. I've got a suite at the Dorchester and everyone's coming back there with me for drinks. Just for a few more drinks!'

Leo laughed. He ushered me out of the club quickly and we got straight into a blacked-out Mercedes – it seemed I had no choice in the matter, and I was having a great time anyway. I realised that, although Leo hadn't accepted no for an answer, his refusal to let me go home wasn't about him getting me back to the hotel. It was about him sharing his night of fun with his friends and me. It was clear that Leo just loved everyone around him to enjoy themselves, and that's what I found so refreshing about him.

When we got up to the hotel suite, there were about twenty of Leo's friends partying there. The suite was huge with a balcony and fantastic view across London. I wandered in and helped myself to a drink. Leo came over, sat next to me and we started chatting on the sofa.

'I'm really enjoying myself tonight, Sofia,' he said during our chat. 'I've got an important day tomorrow with the premiere but I'm having too much fun with my friends to worry about that right now.'

I laughed with him as we talked about London and Brighton. We both loved the sea and I told him how the sea had captured my imagination.

Leo wasn't the Hollywood star that I thought he was going to be – he was really down to earth, open and kind and had absolutely no ego whatsoever. The funny thing was that, when we'd first been introduced in the bar, Leo was a bit shy with me but I found that side of his character really sweet and, as we got drinking, he relaxed a bit more and we got on really well.

It must have been about 4am when Leo finally said that he wanted to go to sleep.

'I'm so tired,' he said wearily. 'Come and see my room. It's massive and there's a secret room.' I followed him into the bedroom, where he opened a wardrobe which led to another room. He got into bed and I sat and chatted to him for a while. Finally, I said that I had to go, kissed him on the cheek and said goodnight.

I didn't know what to do because I didn't want to kiss him or do anything else, but I assumed that was what he wanted. I hadn't kissed a man in years and suddenly felt really nervous.

I sat down on the edge of the bed and Leo joined me. We talked some more and eventually he kissed me on the cheek. His kiss felt amazing, but I didn't want to climb into bed with him, and I hoped he would not ask me to take things further.

'Do you mind if I go home?' I said shyly, breaking away

a little. 'I need to work tomorrow and you said you have to, too.'

'It's fine. You're right.' Leo smiled. 'If you want to come to the premiere tomorrow I'll make sure you get in,' he added.

Everything became a bit rushed after that – it seemed that neither of us was sure about the other, so I made my excuses and left. I rushed out of the room in a bit of a fluster because I felt so overwhelmed by the situation. Leo had been so kind and charming to me that night and I just wanted everything to end clearly between us and on a positive note.

When I got back to my flat, I got into bed and thought about Leo. I thought (perhaps because I had fancied him) that maybe I should have plucked up the courage and been a bit more forward with him. But, as I fell asleep, I felt glad that I'd left the hotel room when I had done. No matter who was interested in me, whether it was an A-list star or a dustman, I wanted to stay single. I wasn't ready to get involved with a man yet – being single was still an important part of me being happy.

The next morning, I woke up and remembered the night before. I was happy about having met Leo. After I'd showered and dressed, I got a call from one of Leo's people.

'You're on the guest list for tonight if you feel like joining us,' said the man.

'Thanks. I'll be there if I can,' I replied, then hung up.

When I left for work, I already knew I wouldn't go that night. I was happy that I'd had a nice encounter with Leo and I wanted to leave it at that. I got on with my day at work and didn't think anything more of it. When I saw Tyrese the next week, he told me that Leo had said I reminded him of the girl in *The Beach*, so I was really very flattered.

Leo inspired me and showed me that talent doesn't need to give rise to ego or over-confidence. His star-like quality was really something to be reckoned with, and our chance meeting was the first step I'd unknowingly taken into an exciting A-list world.

CHAPTER FIFTEEN

IT GIRL

After resolving to inject some fun back into my life, I was soon swept up into a fantastically glamorous and hedonistic London party scene. When I chanced upon an underground, no-holds-barred venue at the end of my road, it was a welcome little surprise.

My work colleagues had told me they'd heard about an amazingly trendy bar near my flat, and every so often they'd ask me to check it out for them. One night, when I needed a well-earned after-work drink, my curiosity got the better of me. I decided to test the waters at The K Bar for myself.

It was getting late, and I couldn't be bothered to dress up, so I wandered down the road in my work suit and blouse. When I reached the bar's entrance, and heard music seeping through the elegant glass-panelled doorway, I held my head up high and eagerly pulled open the door.

'You can't go in unless you're a member,' snapped a surly doorman, waving me out of the way.

I hadn't noticed him and it gave me a bit of a shock. 'I'm sorry, I said, a little embarrassed. 'I didn't see you. I've just moved in down the road and don't know anyone around here. Can I just have one drink at the bar?' I smiled up at him hopefully.

'OK. Because it's only you, I suppose it's fine,' said the doorman before he ushered me through.

The room was decadent in its décor, and heaving with well-dressed men and several glamorous, stunning women. Everyone was smiling, laughing and chatting together, although I couldn't hear much above the loud thumping music. I wandered around for a while, a little unsure of what to do or where to sit, so I decided to stand at the bar. The doorman must have noticed me looking lost and alone at the bar – after a while he came over and said he'd introduce me to a few of the regulars.

'Thanks so much,' I said. 'I'm Sofia by the way.'

The doorman walked me into what looked like the VIP area, and showed me to a table where two well-groomed and handsome men were chatting as they drank champagne Bellinis. When they smiled and welcomed me to join them, I felt safe even though I'd no idea who they were. They had big, welcoming smiles and I remember thinking that they were gay, which is why I initially warmed to them.

I soon discovered that one of the men was a banker called James and the other, Jason, was a fitness instructor to the stars.

'I've just moved into the area and was told to come in here. I've no idea what other bars to try out,' I said. 'I like what I see here, though.' I smiled, and gazed around the packed bar.

'This is the heart of the Chelsea scene,' explained Jason loudly. 'This is where it all happens. You'll fit into this set easily if you're free thinking and like having fun.'

I had no idea what he was talking about. What does he mean by 'scene'? I thought.

'The set consists of fun-loving party people and a mixture of celebrities,' explained Jason as my eyes widened. 'We spend a lot of money together partying, but we're also really generous. We love liberation, but we're also a tight little clique who look after one another.'

I was very intrigued.

'It's hard to get in. The celebrities who mix with us always do so quite happily and freely because of the exclusivity of it all. When you're in, it's highly enjoyable. You'll get looked after impeccably and you won't experience freedom and fun like it anywhere else in the world!'

Jason smiled at me warmly, and I knew straight away that I wanted to embrace this new scene wholeheartedly – a tight-knit, fun-loving and free-thinking family was all I'd ever hoped to be a part of. This was definitely radically different from Gravesend and sounded even better than the social scene in Brighton. When I said goodbye, Jason and James invited me out again the following night, and I couldn't wait!

Whenever I returned to The K Bar after that first night, James and Jason would always be waiting for me, drinks in hand, at their usual table. They happily bought me whatever I wanted to drink and we always had fun together. Over time, they also introduced me to many other regular Chelsea partygoers. I met Arab princes, celebrities, club owners, top models, bankers and trust-fund kids. I noticed that most of them had huge disposable incomes and at first I found that side of the scene quite daunting, but what was so refreshing was that, no matter who or what I was, everyone welcomed and included me in the circle, and I quickly became part of the furniture.

I loved being immersed in the unique and friendly atmosphere of the K Bar – it was such a contrast to the isolation, abuse and restriction I'd experienced in the past. Even the doorman began looking out for me – within two months he'd introduced me to the club's owner, who gave me my own membership! The membership enabled me to get into the place for free every night and to bring guests whenever I wanted.

After a while, I was spending several nights a week in the club, dancing away on the tables and having fun with a vibrant, happy-go-lucky crowd.

'We love you coming in here, Sofia,' the owner often said. 'You help create a great atmosphere. You really get everyone going!' He smiled at me whenever I was dancing away with his clientele, and often told me to help myself to whatever drinks I liked. My heart would fill with joy whenever he complimented me like that – it was so good to have the appreciation of someone who cared.

Sometimes I'd walk into the bar and there'd be a lavish party going on with Dom Perignon on tap. On those occasions, we wouldn't have to spend a thing. The owner was really gifted and generous at throwing these fantastic themed party nights. He'd hire strippers and dancers, and sometimes there would be private strip shows going on in the back. It was all quite decadent and fun. Then, on other nights, the owner would deck the whole place out with white lilies, linen and white furnishings. We'd be served cocktails and champagne by Geisha girls and could have anything that we wished for. For me, those particular nights at the K Bar were always the best and I felt as if I had been transported into another, fairytale-like world.

At this stage, I had a good income from my new job so I could afford to spend money partying with the Chelsea crowd, but I was always careful and practical about my finances. I spent roughly half of my earnings on my music and acting, and the rest on general living expenses and socialising at the K Bar. Sometimes the socialising cost quite a lot, for whenever I went out I loved buying everyone rounds of champagne and cocktails in return for drinks my friends bought for me.

If I had anything left over at the end of the month, I'd treat myself to clothes and beauty treatments – I developed a bit of an obsession with shoes at the time, and would often splash out on pairs of designer shoes by Louis Vuitton or Versace when I could afford to. After all the hard work I was doing, I felt I deserved those things. I'd never had such lovely clothes and shoes before, and I appreciated being able to enjoy them.

I discovered how flamboyant Chelsea really was when I started going to lavish private members clubs like Raffles, Tramps and Annabel's. The Chelsea set would happily spend thousands of pounds whenever they partied at such places. I remember thinking £300 was a lot to spend during a night out, but it soon became normal for me to see someone sharing a good few bottles of vintage Cristal which would have set them back at least £1000. I'd sometimes see as much as £10,000 being totted up at the end of a night, but money was never an issue on the Chelsea scene because everyone just wanted to share whatever they had and have fun.

It was also really refreshing that there were no rules or regulations. Literally anything was possible, it seemed. It didn't matter if a person was 17 years old or 45 years old because, in Chelsea, the night and everyone in it always felt young.

I also started going to private house parties in neighbouring Mayfair. On a typical night out, I'd dance the night away with my friends at Tramp or Annabel's and then go to Vingt Quatre for coffee afterwards. Then we'd all traipse over to whichever house party was being thrown in the area. I remember going to my first house party after I'd been at a local bar called Bardot, a fantastic little cocktail bar which was always great fun. All the usual celebrities loved going in there because it had a private room at the back and the owner was always very discreet.

That night I'd walked into Bardot and noticed Hugh Grant drinking at the bar. I'd seen Hugh out in Chelsea a few times before. He was so nice and polite, despite the fact that he was always surrounded by hundreds of beautiful girls. After we'd chatted together that night, I moved into the thick of the crowd that was swamping the busy bar.

'Who are you?' said a man standing behind me. I turned around and recognised him straight away – it was James Hewitt.

'I'm Sofia. You must be James,' I said confidently.

'We're heading back to my place after this to carry on,' he said, smiling as he handed me his address card. 'I'd love you to stop by. I've heard nice things about you and have seen you about in Chelsea. Please come.'

It turned into a particularly crazy night. When I arrived at James's Chelsea home in the early hours, he took great pride in showing me a furry black hat he'd worn when he'd worked at Buckingham Palace. I remember walking into his living room and thinking how funny it was that James didn't seem to mind his home being filled with what appeared to be complete strangers. But then that was the Chelsea set – no one had a care in the world so long as they could party happily and freely, anywhere and everywhere they were.

That summer, I also began venturing out of town to polo tournaments and horseracing events. The main polo event was, and still is, The Cartier Polo at Great Windsor Park. This meeting is where the Queen presents the cup to the winning polo team. I was so excited when my friend Chris Hayes invited me – I'd heard so much about polo parties, but had never in a million years imagined being able to go to something so lavish.

The day was warm and balmy when Chris collected me from the flat. I'd fretted so much the night before because I'd no idea what to wear but, in the end, I'd opted for a pretty lemon-yellow chiffon Dior dress and a matching pair of heels. I also wore natural make-up and my hair down. After a few hours' drive, we parked the car, wandered into a sea of people, cars and marquees, and moved down on to a huge open lawn where the polo was taking place.

At the far end of the lawn, there was a private members area that was heaving with hundreds of glamorous people and members of the press. I remember feeling slightly overwhelmed by it all as I stood there – I had never been surrounded by such glamour. But I soon got stuck in and, after helping myself to a glass of Pimms, I watched the polo match and began mingling with all the other guests.

Chris and I enjoyed a sumptuous lunch, accompanied by champagne and brandy, in the China White tent. The

London nightclub had put on the lunch and had also organised a party for the night ahead. I got to know Paris Hilton's brother, Nick, which was fun. We sat, huddled together on huge brightly collared cushions, and had coffee. Then, after watching more polo and the Queen presenting the cup, we enjoyed afternoon tea in another huge white marquee. I remember drooling over all the beautiful little iced cakes that were carefully laid out on silver tiered trays, ready to be served up with even more champagne.

At about 7pm, the parties finally started. I was standing outside one of the tents – I'd needed a few minutes of downtime! – when the music kicked off. I looked up and saw thousands of lights and lasers filling the sky. I couldn't believe how beautiful it all was, but the icing on the cake was when I went back inside and met Prince Harry, Mischa Barton and Joshua Hartnett. One of Prince Harry's friends invited me back to a private party they were throwing afterwards but, because I didn't know him, I politely declined the invitation.

Because I enjoyed the Cartier Polo so much, I started going to the horseracing at Ascot. Chris would often get tickets for the Royal Enclosure, which was fantastic because we got to enjoy an amazing first-class service. The first time I went, I met horse owners, fashion designers and society girls and remember thinking how stunning all the men looked in their black top hats, neatly pressed white shirts and grey tails.

I felt such a buzz when I watched my first horserace. The crowd erupted loudly when the race started, but I laughed when it finished because everyone quickly forgot about the fact that they had lost money as they got stuck into their champagne and strawberries again. Ascot was a similar set-up to the Cartier Polo. Chris and I would spend the day socialising, drinking champagne and guzzling strawberries after which we'd party the night away with the usual flamboyant crowd. I also got to wear a fabulous hat and dress, and I absolutely love to dress up. These days, I have my own membership to the Royal Enclosure and love to take friends of mine there who have never been.

Over that summer I became fully immersed in an amazingly happy-go-lucky social scene. Practically overnight, I'd unwittingly become a fun-loving 'It Girl' who everyone wanted around. Becoming an 'It Girl' wasn't something that I'd consciously set out to do – I was just thoroughly enjoying being part of a lifestyle that had been thrown my way, especially because I was able to experiment within it and freely search for 'me'.

The Chelsea scene enabled me to taste life again. These people were successful, happy, thriving personalities and that's exactly what I wanted to be. I no longer felt like the battered Asian girl, and I wasn't a lonely, spotty teenager who had no one to turn to in her hour of need.

The dichotomy between my new life and my old one was incredible. Once I'd been a restricted, abused, poverty-stricken and lonely young Asian factory girl from Gravesend, but by my mid-twenties I'd well and truly escaped my past and was enjoying a free, luxurious and happy new life. I knew that I'd worked hard to get there and that I'd endured so much pain along the way.

Yet I also knew that something much more significant was supporting me during this time. I began to love and uphold my religion more than ever and it played a huge part in my journey. On the face of it, it seemed as if I'd swapped mosques for nightclubs and traded in my family for a crowd of fun-loving party friends, but I was still enjoying Islam whenever and however I wanted to. I continued to love what Islam taught me and, together with my own open and free-thinking mentality, the amazing tools that this religion gave me. I also began to read about other religions such as Christianity and Buddhism and began to realise that they weren't so different after all. Now, I practise Nicherin Daishonin Buddhism. I chant 'Nam myoho renge kyo', which gives me strength and peace. I also go to churches where I pray when I need to.

Chelsea was a totally different world to the one that I'd grown up in, and one where many others from my background wouldn't have felt able to fit in. But because Islam had taught me that no one was above me except God, and that I could be at one with anyone I met, I found it easy to assimilate myself into the scene. No matter how rich, poor, old or young a person was, I knew that anyone could become a friend.

It was around this time that another amazing source of inspiration came into my life and helped guide me on my journey.

CHAPTER SIXTEEN

TV STAR

When I moved to Edith Grove, I met and befriended an old woman called Daphne. Unfortunately, she was very ill with lung cancer, but because of her wisdom, love and the close nature of our relationship, and despite her physical weakness, Daphne always gave me emotional strength and happiness.

Daphne lived down the road from me and, as I spent more and more time caring for her, we became incredibly close. As much as Daphne became like the mother that I'd never had, I in turn became like her daughter, and I looked after her whenever I could. At this time, I still didn't have any contact with my own mother. I often thought about her and carried sadness about what had happened between us, but the happiness of London and Daphne easily compensated for any sad feelings I had about my past.

I made some great friends through Daphne. The most important one was a lovely forty-something celebrity stylist called Alan Keyes. Alan was well respected in his field and was best friends with George Michael and other high-profile celebrities. He had lovely blond hair and sparkly blue eyes, and was always friendly and warm. Daphne and Alan really completed my personal life by giving me the love and support I so craved, and this kept me on track professionally.

Towards the end of that year, I was made redundant, as the company could not afford to keep me on any longer. I was upset when they told me because I was really enjoying my job, but I decided to take a step back and look at all my options. I knew that I could look for another job and continue to try to get acting and singing work in my spare time, or alternatively I could take time off work and focus on my performing again. Because I had enough savings in my account, I opted for the latter. It felt strange and lonely not going into the office every day, but knowing that Daphne was just a stone's throw away always buoyed me up. I felt like I had a little angel in my life that always supported me and made sure that I felt happy.

Whenever I walked down Edith Grove feeling despondent after failing at a casting or an audition, I'd always visit Daphne. She'd be sitting quietly in her tiny, cluttered living room and, after I'd told her the bad news, she would always bolster my confidence.

'You can do it, Sofia,' she always said, reaching for her diary. 'There's always a next time, sweetheart. You're still young and beautiful – and so talented. When's the next casting?'

Daphne kept her diary on the table by her chair and always noted down the dates and purpose of all my auditions. Whenever I watched her scribbling away, my heart was filled with joy – no one had ever shown such an interest in my career. If I wasn't auditioning, I popped in every afternoon anyway. I'd make tea and sit down for a chat. Daphne was so wonderful for my confidence.

'From the moment I saw you, I knew that you were special,' Daphne said, time and time again. 'Someone one day will also see that in you.'

Daphne's support always felt amazing and, because she believed in me, I wanted to do her proud and make her happy. It was her kindness that really made a difference to my progress and, in turn, I always tried to help and love her back.

In the end, due to her illness, Daphne needed more help than Alan and I were able to provide. I did become her legal guardian and undertook many duties such as washing her. I wanted to keep her out of hospital and I managed to persuade the Chelsea Hospital to let Daphne stay at home, where she wanted to die. They sent a nurse to give her 24-hour care.

Sadly, this brought an end to our little jaunts to the Bluebird Café on the Kings Road or to the Chelsea Farmers' Market on a Tuesday afternoon, and I missed those special moments with her incredibly. I did manage to sneak her out from time to time, even when the nurse had said she was too ill to go. Daphne would call me and ask me to come and take her out because the nurse had popped out. I never really knew how long Daphne had left with us, so I would sneak over and take her to feed the birds at Chelsea Harbour. It was worth it to see the smile on her face.

Eventually, Daphne became so ill that she was sent to hospital. I visited her daily and it was shocking seeing her frail body weaken by the day. Daphne's lungs started to fail so they had to insert a tube into her chest and drain off the liquid. All the while, Daphne always kept the smile on her face and the glimmer in her eye.

'George has been in today,' she said one day, smiling up at me from the hospital bed. I knew that she meant George Michael, and I was so glad that he'd made the trip.

That grey November, I celebrated Daphne's last birthday with her in hospital. I bought her a huge bunch of flowers and a teddy and we sat together and tried to sing. Just before I left her bedside Daphne took my hand and pushed a piece of folded paper into it. I put it in my pocket and said goodbye as I watched her shut her eyes. Then Daphne took her last breath and her body became a shell. For a moment it felt like the world had stood still so I took the teddy from her arms and kissed her cheek. I knew Daphne was going to a happy place, but I was still filled with grief.

When I got home, as I undressed I found Daphne's note in my pocket. It was a poem that she'd most probably written when she'd been well enough and had strength.

ENIGMA

Why is the murky river silver?
The overcast sky, pure blue?
Bluebells flower in December
Is it something to do with you?

The sparrow sings like the blackbird
Butterflies rest on the holly
Roses grow on mountain peaks
Nature itself is a folly.

It must be you that has changed the world,
No other person has power
To hold my heart in permanent springtime
My love in perpetual flower.

By Daphne Nicholson... 13.11.1919 – 16.11.2002

That night, as I spent time reading Daphne's beautiful words, I knew that, just as the Chelsea set had shown me freedom and fun, this woman's powerful love had changed my life dramatically. Daphne hadn't replaced my own mother, but she'd shown me a mother's love and I'd never known this existed. Her love made me feel so powerful because it was unconditional and everlasting and I trusted it. As I drifted off to sleep, I felt more determined and exhilarated than ever because Daphne's show of love had given me the final push I needed towards my goals of freedom, success and happiness.

After Daphne's funeral, I put my heart and soul into making it. I'd been given Daphne's wedding ring so I put it on, found a safe place for her poem and worked out what I needed to do. I still wear the ring today, as a reminder of her immense love. She's my guardian angel.

That Christmas, I decided that I needed to get an acting agent. My credentials needed to look professional and meticulous, so I set to work retyping my CV and then put together a covering letter. I arranged for some new, simple, black and white headshots of me to be taken by a photographer, and then spent hours on the Internet researching agents and which ones to contact. As soon as my photos came back I sent off over 100 letters.

When I left the post office that day, I felt like I'd really done Daphne proud. I knew that she'd be looking down on me, and as I walked past where she used to live I remember looking up at the sky and smiling.

I sat around for the next two weeks, waiting for a reply. But, when the postman came each day, there was never any mail for me. I wondered if the lack of interest had something to do with my not having gone to drama school, or if I hadn't had enough luck at the auditions to impress an agent. Whatever the reason, it seemed I was being ignored. It was tough not hearing back from even one person, and I started to wonder if I ever would.

Then, one morning, a letter arrived. It was from an agent called Jennifer Jafreey, and, after all the waiting I'd done, it came as a bit of a surprise. The letter said that she was interested in seeing me. I was so pleased and relieved – I knew from my research that Jennifer was a well-respected and highly talented acting agent, so I called her assistant straight away, hoping to book a meeting for the next morning. I didn't want to waste any time, so it was great when the girl said that Jennifer had a space to see me first thing.

At the time, Jennifer was working from home, so the next morning I went, suited and booted, to her house. Jennifer was very warm and friendly and I remember being struck by her big happy smile and soft features.

'I want to sign you,' Jennifer said after she'd listened to a monologue I'd prepared and read for her. 'I think we could work very well together.'

I was delighted. Jennifer told me she would be in touch and handed me a copy of her contract. I was to go away, read it over and send it back once I'd had a think. I knew I wouldn't need to think too hard, and as we said goodbye

I remember feeling surprised at how quickly the meeting had gone. I was even more surprised that she'd wanted to sign me up so much. Jennifer was the first person who'd really given me a proper chance, and I was so grateful to her. As soon as I got home, I read the contract, signed it and posted it back.

Towards the end of that year, Jennifer secured me my first TV project, a part in a BBC series called *Absolute Power*. The casting was at the BBC studios in White City. Although the character that they had in mind for me was 17 years old, and cockney, I knew that I could easily pull it off.

I felt really confident when I turned up at the studio on the day of the casting. I'd read the script properly and, because the part was a young, funky reporter, I was wearing a colourful T-shirt and trendy-looking skirt. I'd also spent the entire week perfecting the cockney accent. But my nerves got the better of me when I sat down in the waiting area – I noticed that some of the other actresses in the queue looked really beautiful and were much younger that I was. To steady myself, I looked down at Daphne's wedding ring and soon felt my confidence coming back again.

'Sofia Hayat please,' I heard the producer say.

This was it. After kissing Daphne's ring, I walked through the swing doors and into the studio. There were three producers sitting behind a desk, one of whom was holding a script. One of them told me to start. I launched into the part and within half an hour it was over.

I was thrilled when, two days later, I got the call because not only was it a great series to be in, but it was also my first proper acting job. The next week I signed the contract and couldn't believe it when Jennifer told me that they were paying me £600 for each day's work.

I was cast alongside Stephen Fry and played a reporter who worked on a magazine. The filming was over a few weeks and my part was shot at the Cobden Club in North West London. On the first day I was so nervous when I got on the tube to Westbourne Grove. It must have shown because, when I arrived, the man who greeted me promptly told me to sit down and relax.

'Do you want some tea, young lady?' he said, smiling. 'You look so nervous. Sit down here and warm yourself up, love.'

He handed me a cup of steaming hot tea. I was shaking with nerves, but after I'd sipped the tea and went on to the set my nerves quickly disappeared. It was quite strange shooting my first ever TV scene in that club – I'd actually been clubbing in the same place a few years before.

The first few days went really well. As the camera rolled, I kept wanting to pinch myself because I still couldn't believe I had the part. I suppose I still felt insecure because of all the rejections I'd had in the past. However, I managed to do a good job and the production team was really pleased.

I was still partying quite a lot around this time (and enjoying every minute of it!), and things improved even more for me on the work front when I was spotted by a TV producer one night while dancing at Raffles.

A tall Asian man approached me on the dance floor. 'You look fantastic dancing away there,' he said. 'Can you act? Do you have an agent?'

'Well, yes, both!' I replied, smiling. 'Why?'

'We're filming our show in here tonight. Why don't you come over and chat with us.'

'Sure,' I replied. 'I'm Sofia, by the way. I'm an actress.'

He grinned, took my hand and pulled me over to where the cameramen were standing. I watched them wrap up their shoot, and then the producer explained that they were shooting a piece about the London club scene that was to be aired on Zee TV later that week. I said I was looking for work and the producer pressed his card into my hand.

'We have to move on now to another club, but please call me. I think I might have something you'd be really interested in.'

Once they had gone, I stood at the side of the dance floor feeling shocked and excited because out of the blue someone had spotted me.

To cut a long story short, the next week I was signed up as the main presenter on Zee TV! I was to work on *Sorted*, their brand-new entertainment show. They only paid me a small amount per show, but I was so happy to be finally working regularly and earning money again.

The show was a great concept and was so perfect for me. I had to dash around London and the north of England at night and film in nightclubs and bars. Some nights we'd hit high-profile clubs and other nights we'd venture into smaller student ones where we'd film the punters and interview them dancing together and having fun. Regardless of where we were, the job was amazing fun and very rewarding.

I think my style of dress was one of the reasons I went down so well on screen. Because I had to buy my own clothes for each show, and because I wanted to make an impact, I struck up a deal with a fantastic boutique on the Kings Road. I went there once a week and selected clothes that were one-offs, then wore them out for the night. If I didn't wear an amazing outfit from there, I'd work out specific themes for each shoot. One night, I dressed up as a schoolgirl and acted like a kid throughout the whole show. Another time, I hired a flamboyant Victorian dress with a huge, curly white wig. It was really eccentric and huge fun. We definitely got noticed because we got some fantastic footage with the punters.

The best thing was that, over time, I started to make an impact on the Asian market and ratings soared. After six months, the show had become a huge success across the Asian network. I lasted on that show for almost three years, and eventually the show had 500,000 viewers a week in the UK, and over 4 million in Africa and Europe. I became a known face on Asian TV and began to travel the world, helping to promote the network and my show in India, Africa and all over Europe.

I had fans stopping me in the street wherever I went and began receiving huge amounts of fan mail. I set up a website so that I could handle everything quickly and efficiently and was soon getting up to 20,000 hits a week. I loved it that people were going on to my message board to discuss cultural and religious issues that I was obviously very familiar with. I loved being a sounding board and, above all, I loved being able to help other Asians who seemed to be suffering from the same problems as I'd suffered.

I received lots of amazing emails from young Asian women seeking advice on how to get into the business, but there were many touching emails from young women who wrote to me in desperation, having been, or being, forced to marry someone they didn't want to. They always asked me how I'd got to where I was, and I was pleased to become a role model for Asian girls. I wanted to help in any way I could.

Unfortunately, there was a backlash against me towards the end of my time on the show. It came predominantly from the Asian community. They were upset that an Asian woman was appearing on television wearing short skirts and going to clubs.

'We've seen your show, Sofia. Everyone thinks you're a disgrace,' my sister told me one day during a heated phone call.

Saira and I had kept in touch intermittently over the years. We were still close, although we never spoke about my parents.

'I don't care, Saira,' I said. 'I'm happy in my life but I'm even happier now because I'm making an impact. Things need to change.'

And that was that. Saira couldn't argue with what I had said, and she knew no one in my family could deter me any more.

I even received death threats on my website. They were all fairly similar: *You should be ashamed of yourself being a Muslim. Muslim women do not do what you do. You will be killed for showing your body.* After reading the same words day after day, I knew full well that those sorts of messages were mainly empty threats from younger viewers who had nothing better to do and needed an outlet for their anger. I'd already faced death at the hands of my own mother, so these threats really didn't bother me at all. Sometimes, I'd get nicer emails from young Muslims trying to tempt me back to 'The right path of Allah'. These people thought I needed their help, but I can't say I was tempted to accept it!

In the light of all this, I remember doing a live show at Wembley Stadium and expecting to be shunned by the audience. I was scared that someone would hurt me after I'd performed on stage, and feared that parents would be nasty to me because of the way I looked. However, much to my delight, as I entered the stadium, I was surrounded by parents asking for my picture.

I was wearing a short skirt, made of gold silk, and a matching bra top. The skirt had a beautiful fuchsia-pink train embedded with stones of various colours. I'd wanted to bring the East-West influence into my clothes in a young funky way, and I think it worked. The crowd erupted when my name was called and I went on stage with my dancers. The atmosphere that night was electrifying.

I remember spinning on stage and catching a glimpse of myself on the huge cinema screens. It was so overwhelming because, halfway through my performance, the crowd went completely crazy and chanted, 'One more, Sofia! One more, Sofia!' The trouble was I'd only prepared one song, so I ran off the stage and hugged the dancers, thanking them for helping me put on an amazing performance.

As I left the stadium, some of the parents were waiting for me and began grabbing me because they wanted their picture taken with their children and me. I felt like an army had descended upon me. 'Sign this, Sofia! We thought you were fantastic fun. You look so strong and confident! Please let us take a picture with you!' they cried.

I must have signed over 400 autographs that evening and I felt truly fantastic. For the first time in years, I felt attached to my culture again. Both children and parents seemed to like me and want me by their sides. It was as if I was being welcomed back into their world. The backlash had died down, and the show continued to flourish.

CHAPTER SEVENTEEN
HOLLYWOOD STARS

Whether I was out filming *Sorted*, or enjoying a night out with my friends, I was suddenly mixing with plenty of celebrities, and had some amazing encounters along the way. I attended all sorts of glamorous showbiz events and star-studded parties, but most of all I loved attending all the West End film premieres. They were dazzling events, and made me feel like I'd been transported into a totally different world.

I'd spend days deciding what to wear. Sometimes I'd design something special and get it made up by a local Chelsea seamstress, then team up the outfit with an expensive pair of shoes or a stylish designer handbag. Other times, I'd select a swish designer dress from Harrods, or fly to Milan and shop my socks off in all the fashionable little designer boutiques.

Whenever there was a film premiere, I always had butterflies in my stomach when I set off for Leicester Square. If I wasn't filming the event for *Sorted*, I'd stand confidently on the red carpet in front of the paparazzi so that they could snap away and frantically ask me questions about what I was up to, who I was dating, or who designed my dress. Often they'd ask me why I wasn't working – the paps knew me as a presenter for *Sorted*, so we'd always laugh and joke together whenever I wasn't working alongside them in the media pen.

Over time, I became familiar with the red-carpet routine but, whichever side of the media pen I was on, those moments were never boring. Because I always had so much adrenalin running through my body, I always found it hard sitting still when the actual film started.

The first film premiere I ever went to was *Alexander*, in Leicester Square and that night I was shooting for *Sorted*. I wanted to stand out and get a good interview with Colin Farrell, the lead, and, because I knew that there would be hundreds of other reporters on the red carpet with me, I knew that I had to find a way to make sure that Colin spoke to me. I needed to try to stand out. In the end, I plumped for a pretty pink sparkly dress, matching Dior heels and natural make-up. I wanted to create a lasting impression on Colin, so to get a feel for his character I spent the night before the premiere on the Internet, poring over all the interviews Colin had done over the past few years.

I met up with my film crew on the night, and we were quickly herded into the media pen to wait for the talent to arrive. Luckily, my team were at the front and we spotted Colin first. I noticed him striding towards me wearing a white shirt and black trousers (oh, and his hair was long and really messy!), then, just as I'd hoped, Colin skipped all the other reporters and came straight up to me!

'Are you interviewing me?' he asked, smiling.

'Yes, I'm Sofia Hayat for Zee TV. Do you prefer sex or making love, Colin?' I asked him quickly, looking straight into his eyes. I knew that my question was suggestive, and that I was supposed to ask him about the film, but I'd done my homework and knew full well that Colin loved being cheeky. The night before I'd read an interview where Colin had mentioned that he preferred to have sex. So, naturally, that was what I asked him about.

I heard laughter behind me – the other journalists had heard my question.

'Oh, I prefer making love,' Colin said, grinning.

Everything was going swimmingly because I got the exact response that I'd wanted. To top it off, Colin went further and kissed me on the cheek! 'Cheeky f***er,' he added, and wandered off towards the cinema with a rather perturbed film publicist at his side.

After that, we set to work preparing for Angelina Jolie's arrival. Angelina was only about a metre away from me and I was just about to speak to her, when things sadly backfired on me. I hadn't noticed but, when I'd been speaking to Colin, Angelina's publicist had been standing right behind him and had overheard what I'd said. He was a small, thin man in a grey suit with spiky hair.

'Angelina won't be talking to you tonight,' he said, 'and there won't be any interviews after the film now.'

My heart sank because I'd bought Angelina's son a teddy and wanted to give it to her after the film. I also felt guilty – because of what I'd done, my crew wasn't allowed to get any more footage. To make matters worse, all the other media interviews were then banned!

'It's OK, Sofia,' a BBC journalist said, trying to comfort me. 'Colin was having fun. He loves questions like that.'

I felt a little better. And, although things had gone wrong that night, the upside was that Colin would remember me. A year or so later, the *Miami Vice* film premiere and after-party were taking place in London, and I'd been invited as a guest by one of the film's publicity girls. I hadn't seen Colin since the *Alexander* furore and I didn't expect for one minute that he'd notice me if I showed up at his premiere and after-party.

I went to the premiere with my friend Dawn. I paraded up the carpet and was quit taken by the palm trees that were dotted along the path to the cinema. It was great fun, and the press took lots of pictures of me as I posed away. On the way back home, I decided to stop by at the Sanderson Hotel, where the official after-party was being held, for a quick drink. I was wearing a see-through vintage black lace dress, and had done my hair to one side in curls, so I felt really good when I wandered into the swish hotel bar.

I wandered around for a while but couldn't see anyone I knew. I was about leave, and, as I went to walk out towards reception, I heard a voice say, 'Hey, you!' I turned around and there stood Colin, smiling at me. 'It's the cheeky TV girl,' he exclaimed, laughing. 'You're not leaving already, are you?'

'Hello, Colin. So I didn't upset you then?' I said.

'No, not at all. I thought it was quite funny. Have you got any more cheeky questions for me tonight then?'

'Angelina's not around, is she?' I said, and we giggled together.

I was pleased that Colin was fine with me after what had happened. As we stood drinking at the bar together, we laughed about it even more. Annoyingly for him, Colin was kept busy fighting off several busty blondes who were trying to muscle their way between us as we chatted. When they started coming at him from all directions, he was surprised – although he came across as confident, he appeared quite flustered by it all.

'At least they don't ask you annoying questions,' I joked. 'Just pretend you're with me.' I knew full well how to defuse situations that involved swooning women. 'Let's pretend we are in deep conversation about something ... see, it's already working,' I said, laughing.

As I'd anticipated, the blondes smirked, gave up the chase and slunk off into the back of the bar area to try it on with someone else.

Colin smiled at me. 'Thanks, Sofia,' he said. 'They probably can't even string a sentence together. I'd much rather stand here and talk to you anyway.'

We carried on chatting and just kept laughing. When we finally stopped, I asked Colin about the *Alexander* premiere again. I still wasn't sure if I'd offended him. 'In all seriousness, I'm sorry about what happened,' I said. 'I hope everything was OK after they stopped all the other interviews because of what I'd said.'

'Oh come on,' he said. 'I didn't care about the question at all and I felt bad that everything was cancelled because of it. It was really unnecessary.'

I felt much better after that. We went on to enjoy more cocktails together while dancing away to Prince with all the other *Miami Vice* cast members around us.

The same year, I also got to know Will Smith after we met at the premiere for *Men In Black II*. My producers hadn't asked me to cover the film, so I decided to go along and just relax. I chose to wear a gold skirt and top with a plunging fuchsia wrap. The wrap was covered in see-through Indian trimmings and, although the finished outfit looked expensive, I made it for £40. I felt a million dollars when I finished getting ready and couldn't wait to get on to the red carpet.

At this time, the British Asian media paid attention to me whenever I showed up on the red carpet. The British press knew me as well, but more as a reporter. With that in mind, I really wasn't prepared for the reaction I got that night when I arrived at the cinema and stepped out of my car.

I began walking towards the cinema, said hello to a couple of reporters from the Asian networks, and then passed Will Smith, who was busy chatting away to a BBC reporter. Just after I got past Will, the atmosphere exploded behind me. I suddenly heard all the British media asking one another who I was, so I turned and nervously flashed a smile.

'What's your name?' they shouted. 'We know you from somewhere.' Their cameras set off what seemed like a million flashes.

'Sofia Hayat,' I shouted. 'I'm a TV presenter. I often cover these film events so that's why you might have seen me before. Tonight I've left my microphone at home!'

'You look amazing,' some of them said. 'Can we get some more shots of you afterwards?'

'Of course. See you later.' I smiled and headed towards the entrance, hoping that the excitement over me hadn't diverted any attention away from Will.

Once inside, I bumped into ex-footballer John Fashanu. I'd met John through friends of Naomi Campbell and we'd kept in touch. 'Are you up for the after-party, Sofia?' John said to me as we stood chatting. 'I can't go tonight, but I want you to have my ticket.'

I accepted the ticket and thanked John, promising to buy him drinks at the next party.

During the film, I remember feeling really tired and unsure about going to the party, especially since I was alone. But, when I saw all the other celebrities filtering out of the cinema and chatting about the party, I couldn't resist! The party was at Sketch – a bar and restaurant on Conduit Street that was 'the' place to go in London back then – and I'd always wanted to see what it was like.

It was buzzing inside Sketch. I could tell that the place was heaving with celebrities because I could pick out all the members of the cast and there was security everywhere. Ahead of me was a small white stone stairwell that led down to the restaurant, and at the back of the restaurant was the VIP area. It was a dome-shaped, cave-like space with a bar at the centre.

'It's straight ahead,' said the security man. 'Leave your coat at the check and go straight through.'

Inside the restaurant, the lavish party was in full swing. There was a huge dance floor and waitresses walking around with trays of champagne and lovely canapés of sushi and tiny burgers. At the back of the dance floor was a small, cocoon-like bar. The music was R & B and they were playing Will Smith tracks, of course.

I was happily sipping a cocktail when one of the female cast members, Naomi Harris, came up to me and complimented me on my outfit. She was tall and black and had long black hair and was so friendly. 'Why don't you come and join the rest of the cast in the back room for drinks?' she said after we'd chatted for a bit. 'You'll get on with everyone like a house on fire.' She took my hand and pulled me towards the private room. 'That outfit will definitely be the talk of the town tonight,' she added.

As we paraded across the dance floor and into the other room, I noticed so many heads turning to watch us. I don't know why she had singled me out, but I felt really special.

Once in the bar, I spotted Will Smith sitting in the corner. He looked up, smiled at the girl and waved us over. Everything was happening so quickly that it was hard to catch my breath, but within seconds I was sitting down right next to Will. He was just how I'd imagined him to be. He was constantly smiling and friendly and we got on straight away. 'I saw you before the film, didn't I?' he said. 'And what's the deal in this place – are the bathrooms supposed to be eggs?'

We both laughed. I explained who I was and then Will joked that the toilet had spoken to him when he'd opened the door. The décor is quite flamboyant in Sketch and all the loos look like big white eggs. Sometimes music is played in the egg-like toilets, which is why he thought they were talking to him.

In the back bar, we had lots of privacy and no one came and bothered Will, but, as soon as we moved through into the main room, people kept coming up to him to chat with him. I could see that he wanted to oblige and please everyone, but that he also wanted to have some space and down time. After a while, he looked really tired and said that he wanted to leave.

'Let's all go back to the hotel and have a quiet drink there. It's been a long night,' he said, looking at me.

I nodded, unsure of whether to go or not, but, after he told the other guests what the new plan was, we all left the dance floor together, got our coats and clambered into a couple of blacked-out cars outside. The paparazzi snapped me but Will was careful not to have his picture taken with anyone.

As we sped off to the Mandarin Hotel, I couldn't believe I was sitting in a car with Will Smith and his best friend. It was the last thing I had expected to happen, and it was great. Will was so warm and friendly and I felt so relaxed. The conversation flowed until we spotted even more paparazzi waiting on the pavement outside his hotel.

'I'll need you two to get out first,' Will said nervously, as we approached the hotel entrance. 'I'll stay in the car and I'll meet you in the bar in a bit.'

His best friend and I got out of the car and went in to wait for Will at the bar. It was about 3am and I was also starting to feel really tired by then.

'I think I'm going to go to bed,' I said when Will finally joined us.

'Come on, Sofia,' said Will, smiling. 'I drove around the hotel three times and now you're going! Come on, have just one drink for the road.'

I was really tired, and knew I had to leave. 'I'm sorry,' I said. 'I've had such a fantastic night, but I need some sleep. Thanks so much, though.'

Will was too much of a gentleman to pressure anyone into anything, and said he understood. I knew that I'd see them all again when they next came to London, so I didn't feel as if this meeting would be the last. I felt so special in their company that night, and woke up the next day beaming. I beamed even more when I looked on the Internet and discovered that my fuchsia pink and gold paparazzi shots were being distributed all over the world!

Will and I met up again at a Prince's Trust lunch, which

was held in conjunction with the UK release of *The Pursuit Of Happyness*, another one of his films. That evening I met Will's wife Jada and their son, Jaden, who stars with his dad in the film. I saw how in love with them he is.

'Are you coming to the premiere tonight?' Will asked me after the meal. 'Absolutely!' I said, but it was hard to have a proper conversation at the meal because Will was surrounded by swarms of excited fans who all wanted a small piece of him.

I caught his eye as he signed autograph after autograph and then posed for pictures. As he glanced over at me I remember thinking how awesome he was. On the surface Will is funny and giving, the character we all see on screen and love, but, if you take him away from the crowds, he is quieter, deep and understated. That dichotomy only proves how professional and talented he really is.

Around this time, I also met and partied with another huge star. Again, it was my dress which captivated her and created a stir. In 2003, I started hanging out at a trendy Chelsea bar called The Collection. It was always heaving with celebrities and media types, and I knew the owner, Jag, so loved relaxing in there with him whenever I'd filmed my show.

One night, Jag and I were enjoying a glass of champagne at the bar, when he invited me to Mariah Carey's birthday party, which he was hosting at the bar the following Saturday. I had a hard week ahead, and Mariah's party sounded like a great way to end it.

'Count me in,' I said.

On the Saturday, the first thing I noticed when I walked into the bar was that Mariah Carey looked *so* stunning. She was dressed up as a mermaid and, as you can imagine, everyone's eyes were out on stalks. Her long, silky hair and gorgeous figure were breathtaking. I spotted Jag behind the bar but he seemed busy so I helped myself to a drink and went to find a seat in the corner, where I knew the music always sounded better. But someone interrupted on my way to the corner.

'You look great,' I heard an American woman say.

I turned and saw Mariah Carey walking towards me. I thought she'd probably mistaken me for someone else, but before I could say anything she smiled and asked me where I'd bought my dress. 'Is the designer British?' she added.

'Well, yes, she's British. I designed it myself. I'm Sofia Hayat,' I replied, holding out my hand to her. 'Happy Birthday.'

I twirled around so Mariah could get a proper look.

'Your dress is really something special,' she said.

'Thanks, Mariah,' I said, holding up my champagne glass. 'Enjoy your evening.'

Mariah wandered off and I suddenly felt a hand snaking around my waist. I turned around again!

'I agree with Mariah,' a man said, smiling at me.

I recognised the face immediately – it was Matt Goss. Some of the other girls at school had been massively into Bros, so I recognised him straight away.

'You stand out a mile,' he said, his baby-blue eyes boring into mine. 'What did you say your name was?'

'I'm Sofia,' I replied, running my fingers up and down my empty champagne glass. Matt still had his hand on my waist, and I felt a flutter of excitement right where he was touching me.

'And what does Sofia do with herself these days?' Matt asked flirtatiously.

'At the moment I present a TV show,' I replied.

'Well, your glass looks empty. Let me fill it up, and then I want to hear all about it.' He took my hand and led me towards the crowded bar.

That night we chatted and chatted and soon became unaware of what was going on around us. I quickly forgot about Mariah Carey and how she'd noticed my dress, and I didn't even see the members of Westlife come in. I told Matt about my show and how I'd made it a success and he chatted about his comeback and future plans. Matt ordered another bottle of champagne and we both got stuck in.

In the end, Matt and I exchanged numbers and I left. I was feeling a bit tipsy and light headed from all the excitement so just wanted to get home and curl up in my bed. When I'd undressed and was about to go to sleep my mobile bleeped. It was Matt. 'You looked stunning tonight, Sofia. When are we meeting?' said the text.

'Soon. I'm just going to sleep,' I replied.

Although I'd tried to take control of the contact between us, Matt persisted and rang me the next day, asking me to come and see him.

Matt lived near Sloane Square and, because it was almost lunchtime, he promised to get a sandwich for me and have it ready and waiting. I'd had a casting that morning so I made my way over there afterwards. Matt's flat was old in style and, although he was just renting it, it was cosy.

I wasn't nervous at all when I walked into his living room. I was just looking forward to chatting to him over lunch. He gave me the sandwich he'd bought from Harvey Nichols and then got his guitar to play me one of his new songs as I ate. Then, without a moment's warning, he stopped playing, sat down next to me on the sofa and kissed me softly. I was worried because I thought I must have tasted of grilled aubergine!

Matt didn't seem to mind, though, and after he stopped kissing me he smiled and ran his fingers through my hair and down my neck. His eyes were piercing blue and I started to tingle all over as he kissed me again. I hadn't felt like that in years. It was bizarre because so many girls I'd known in my late teens had loved Bros and there I was being kissed by Matt Goss on his living-room sofa!

Matt's mobile rang during our kissing session and he had to get ready for a meeting. We said our goodbyes and, although I wasn't sure where it would go, I felt warm as I rushed home to Edith Grove. I had felt butterflies in my tummy again and that was a huge step for me. I didn't think Matt and I would work, but I'd been lifted up by him and that was enough. We'd shared a nice moment together and I will never forget being kissed by Matt Goss and him telling me that I was beautiful!

Towards the end of 2003, I felt on top of the world. I was excelling as a TV presenter and meeting and being inspired by all sorts of talented film and music stars. Being around such artists was so uplifting and I was always comforted that there were like-minded people out there who understood my passion. We were on the same journey, after all, and being a part of their thrilling world always brought out the best in me. It was during those moments that I knew that God was still looking after me, and that on that cold night a decade ago, when I'd faced my mother on Brighton pier, I'd chosen the right path.

CHAPTER EIGHTEEN
BOLLYWOOD STAR

Despite delving into the celebrity world, and wanting to spend more and more time in it, I wouldn't allow myself to be sidetracked. It was always tempting when yet another party or premiere invitation fell through my letterbox, but my ambition always got the better of me and I often turned things down. It had been fine partying hard and networking when I was at the recruitment company in the City, and when I'd started *Sorted*, but now I wanted more and I knew that some things needed to give.

I desperately wanted to take on more TV roles, and I'd also set my sights on winning a part in a full-length feature film. When the chance to appear in an Asian reality TV show called *Bollywood Star* cropped up in 2004, I jumped at it.

Bollywood Star was to be aired on Channel Four over three months. The programme was a competition and the winner would get a part in a Bollywood film. It all sounded so fantastic. When I read what sort of talent they wanted,

I thought it sounded just up my street. I immediately sent off all my details, including my photo and CV. I couldn't wait to hear back.

Then I received a polite letter from the producers asking if I could call the production assistant to arrange a meeting as soon as I was free. I called straight away. But, instead of arranging a date to meet, they did something most surprising – they told me that they wanted to start filming me the next week!

'We want you at the first round of studio auditions up in Birmingham,' said the assistant producer. 'You'll need to formulate your own dance routine and do your own styling. It has to be Bollywood flavoured.'

'Don't you want to meet me first before we start filming?' I asked. I was worried that they might not like me, and I didn't want to waste their time.

'We know who you are and it's fine. We definitely want you to be a part of the first audition rounds.' She explained that further auditions would be held, after which six finalists would be flown off to India for the final round. 'A proper feature-film contract lies at the end of the road for the winner,' she added. 'You'll do well.'

And that was that.

I had decided to quit *Sorted* so I knew the timing for *Bollywood Star* was perfect. The last few shows that I'd done had been a bit crazy and, because the show was so popular, whenever I went out filming I was getting mobbed. It wasn't safe any more. It was a hard decision – I didn't wanted to let my fans down – but my safety had to come first and I handed in my notice.

I began focusing on *Bollywood Star* and set to work preparing for the Birmingham audition. I wanted to do something really unique, so I found a Kathak dancer and gave her a week to train me in this traditional Asian style of dance. I chose Kathak because it featured in old, classic Bollywood movies, which I love. I also saw it as a great opportunity to learn a beautiful new dance form.

I also knew that I needed to hone my acting skills, but I knew the audition would require improvisation, so there wasn't much work I could do on that in the time available. I'd already done an A level in Theatre Studies and a three-year degree in Performing Arts, and I had acting experience, so I was quietly confident on that front. Because I'd already trained so hard, and because I had such passion, I suppose I just hoped that I'd do well.

Finally, I had to make sure I looked the part. I wanted to slim down a bit, so I began following a strict, healthy diet of fruit and vegetables with lots of lean protein, and I didn't eat after 6 pm. I had my mind set on designing my own outfit because I wanted to look as sexy as possible while fusing old and new Bollywood styles.

I felt fully prepared when I travelled up to Birmingham. I was pretty nervous, but two of my Chelsea friends were really kind and supportive. They even offered to drive me there and wait for me outside the audition room.

'You'll be fine, Sofia. You'll win!' said Federica warmly, while my other friend Chris hugged me tightly outside the audition room.

'You look stunning,' he said, smiling.

When I looked down at my outfit, I felt it. I ran my fingers through my glistening, sleek hair – it set off my new, slimmer figure really well. As I stood there with my two best friends, I thought of the times I'd stood alone at Pineapple Studios in Covent Garden all those years ago.

Back then, I'd had no support and had felt so alone. I had been rejected time and time again. Now, though, I had the support of my friends, but I was still really nervous and scared. I'd prepared so hard for this moment, and I didn't want to let my friends down.

It was time to go in.

I stood in front of the three judges in the audition room and thought of Chris and Federica listening and praying for me outside the door, and then I thought of Daphne watching over me. Without saying a word, one of the female judges waved and the track I'd chosen to sing and dance began to play. I was thrown slightly because I wasn't ready to start, but I had no choice but to get on with it and give it my all.

The routine went so quickly, but I enjoyed every minute of it and it must have shown. 'That was really great, Sofia,' said the male judge. 'We'd like you to come back for the semi-finals in a few weeks' time. How do you feel about that?'

The TV cameras were still rolling

'I thought it was fantastic! I would love so much to come back! Thank you, thank you!' I said, and left the room.

I made it through the second round of *Bollywood Star*, and the six finalists (one of them being me!) were told that we'd be flown off to India for the final. There was Rupak, Rivona, Sador, Ricky, Heidi and myself and I really couldn't wait.

Before we flew, we all had to do the necessary presswork that we'd signed up for in our contracts. Although I'd been excited about that side of things too, it was during the presswork that various problems and uncertainties started to arise. I had guessed that I had been chosen for

Bollywood Star because I had a profile, but what I didn't realise was that the producers intended to capitalise on my tragic, and therefore newsworthy, past.

'We want you to be the sexy, confident one,' said the producer when I called her about my photoshoot and interview. 'That can be reflected in your pictures. In the interview, we want you to talk about how you've succeeded after your family disowned you. It's a very strong and inspirational story, and relevant to the whole Bollywood dream.'

I told her I didn't mind talking about my past. After all, how I followed my dream might help other women out there, I thought. 'But I don't want to go into too much detail about my family because it might upset them,' I stressed.

I was willing to talk openly about how I'd got to where I was, and how strong and independent I felt, but I didn't want to dredge up anything else, especially if my parents might eventually read about it. I still cared for and loved them after all. But unfortunately the show's producers had already started their own process of speaking to my family without my knowing.

I went all out for the photographer on the day of the photoshoot. We shot in a studio in north London and I dressed in a sexy Lengha – an Indian skirt – and a top that showed off my midriff. I was pleased with the Polaroids, and when we finished they told me that they'd send everything out to the national press the next week. And sure enough, there I was the following week, splashed across the tabloids as the sexy *Bollywood Star* girl. It was an exciting start for me.

After the photoshoot, and a week before we flew to

India, the camera crew came to my flat to film and interview me. I was fine chatting about how I'd changed my life and had found freedom to perform and follow my dreams. However, when the cameras stopped rolling, one of the producers began asking me more personal questions, especially about my mother, and I burst into tears.

'Wait, let's get this on camera,' he said quickly.

What happened next really shook me up. A few days later, my sister Saira rang and told me that the producers had contacted her to get my mother's home number.

'I didn't want to give it to them, Sofia, but they were really persuasive and said that it would help you win the competition,' she explained bashfully. 'I gave it to them. They've contacted Mum and asked her to come to the semi-finals.'

I felt so angry as Saira went on to explain that my mother had gone mad when they'd called her and had asked them to leave her alone. I was so shocked by what Saira was telling me because I also knew that they'd planned for me to show my body on stage during the semi-finals. It was awful to think that this might happen right in front of my mother without my even knowing she was there.

Having my mother in the audience would have made great TV, but I don't know what I would have said or done if she had been there. I think it would have pushed me over the edge – not only would Mum have walked out feeling humiliated and upset, but also I would have been transported back to feeling like the disappointing child.

Looking back, I think that my reaction to this incident proved that, deep down, I wanted to see my mother again – I was just upset that someone else had taken the step for me and without my consent. It was such a sensitive issue for me because of what I'd been through with my mother since we'd separated, and because *I* wanted to be the one who found the strength to contact her. I wanted to be able to make that special choice when the time was right for me – and also for her.

That night, I thought long and hard about everything. At first, I didn't want to carry on with the show because I felt the producers had crossed the line, but as the hours ticked by I changed my mind. I'd signed a contract, after all, and had been keen to do it because of the experience and exposure that I'd get. I thought hard about what might lay ahead for me in my career – I certainly didn't want things with my family to get in the way of performing again. I knew that, if I didn't take control of things for myself, everything could fall to pieces again like it had so many years ago.

After a night of tears and deep thought, I decided to knuckle down and stay the journey. I knew my mother was angry, yet felt relieved that she wouldn't be coming to the show. It felt strange knowing that someone else had communicated with my mother about me, and I wondered what she really thought and felt after they called her. I wondered if she missed me. Did she want to see me again or was she still consumed with anger about me?

We'd separated eight years beforehand and, even though she was still my mother, we'd become relative strangers. I had no idea about her and her thoughts, but I still hoped in my heart that my mother might one day find some compassion and change.

Despite the rocky start, I joined the flight to India. When

we arrived, we were put up in a hostel called Anand Hall which was OK. It wasn't luxurious, but my room was comfortable with just a bed, shower and a toilet, though the grey cement walls in the bathroom got to me after a while. I would be more than glad to leave when we finished two weeks later!

We had an early start on the first morning. After breakfast, we were briefed about the two-week stay and told what was expected of us. Our days had been planned out and packed with stunt and acting training, and we would be put in different and challenging situations to see how well we coped as individuals.

Over the next week, I was filmed during acting classes and stunt training, which I really enjoyed. My challenge was filmed on a building site, where I had to carry cement on my head and tip it on to an excavated foundation. It was really hard work but I think I managed it well. I was really exhausted but, after the shoot, I went over and spoke with a group of kids who lived on the building site with their parents. I'd noticed them standing in the dust and dirt when we'd arrived in the morning, and throughout the shoot all I had wanted to do was speak to them and ask how they were.

'How old are you?' I asked one of the little girls. She was so beautiful and innocent, and she told me that she didn't know. I felt really sad when she'd said this, so I sat with her for an hour and tried to work out her age for her. When we'd decided that she must have been 12 years old, she smiled up at me and thanked me.

'Come and eat with us,' she said, taking my hand and pulling me towards a corrugated iron hut. But as we walked together the producers told me not to go in case I got sick.

'It's fine,' I said. 'I want to share a meal with her.' So I went and sat with her in the hut. I watched as the older women handed her a tiny plate of dry chapatti and vegetable curry, which wouldn't have filled a mouse. I told her I couldn't take her food –there was so little of it.

'Oh, please just taste it,' she replied. 'I want to share with you because you told me my age.'

The producers kept telling me not to eat it, that I would get sick, but I didn't care. I ate a few spoonfuls and shared water from her cup and she told me how the food had been cooked in the earth with wood from the trees. The food didn't fill my stomach and it was stale and old, but I ate it because I didn't want them to feel like I thought I was better than them. I just wanted the girl to feel – at least for one moment – that we were at one, and equal in the world, and that I was happy to share anything with her if it made her happy.

Unfortunately, I did get really ill, but it was worth it. The producers didn't film that part of my day, but I didn't care because the little girl and I knew what we had shared together, and that meant more than anything to me. I'll always remember that moment and will cherish the pictures I took the day I sat with the little Indian girl in her corrugated iron shelter. The experience taught me so much.

They were working for such little money, ate so little and lived in shanty houses on the building site. Wearing just flip-flops and saris, they were working in such dangerous conditions without hard hats and it seemed so far removed from the life I was living back home. Those moments were heartbreaking, but I also discovered something even more telling while I was in India.

As I came face to face with the Bollywood 'casting

couch' phenomenon, I realised exactly why my mother had feared and reviled the performing world so much, and why she'd assumed Omar was telling the truth about me being a prostitute in Brighton. The bottom line is Bollywood is very competitive and in more cases than not, the girls and the boys are expected to compromise themselves. I learned this first hand by experiencing something very horrible while I was there.

One day a message had been left for me at Anand Hall by the stunt co-ordinator we'd trained with. I called him straight back. He told me a director wanted to see me to discuss a film project that evening after filming. 'Make sure you look presentable and radiant at the meeting,' he added. 'You know what they're like – look sexy.'

'I wonder why they want to see me?' I said to Rupak, one of the semi-finalists I had become friendly with, as I sat in her room.

'Maybe they want to offer you a part in another film,' she said. 'I'd go and make an impression if you can.'

I was prepared to look radiant and to work hard in my career in order to make it, but I wasn't prepared to do what was about to be asked of me. If I'd known what was going to happen, I wouldn't have turned up to the meeting in the first place.

After filming that day, I showered and dressed in a plain, knee-length skirt and fitted top. It was a nice look, but it wasn't overtly sexy. I felt fine when I looked at my reflection in the mirror, but as the time of the meeting approached I started to feel uneasy about seeing this director in the evening, and at his home.

'Ricky, will you come with me to this meeting tonight? Something's bothering me. Do I look OK?' I said.

'You look perfect, and of course I'll come with you. I can wait outside. He's an important man, Sofia. He has apparently worked with the best.'

Ricky smiled at me reassuringly as we walked towards a waiting rickshaw on the road outside the hotel. Ten minutes later, we were parked up outside a huge white mansion. We paid the driver and wandered through the gates to the front door. A petite maid showed us into what must have been the parlour. As we walked through the hallway I noticed how luxurious everything was. The floor was an expensive cream marble and the hallway seemed to carry on for miles.

'Miss Hayat, I'll let him know you're here,' said the maid, and then she vanished through a door to the side of the exquisitely furnished room.

'Will you wait here, Ricky,' I said quietly. 'I feel fine to go in alone. I'm just nervous because this could be my big break.'

Ricky hugged me and wished me luck. When the maid returned and told me to follow her, I kissed him on the cheek and left him behind.

As I entered the director's room, I saw him sitting on a huge leather chair. He was unprepossessing, and he smiled as I walked towards him.

'Oh yes, you're pretty,' he said. 'And your figure is beautiful. I rarely see curves like this on Asian actresses.'

'Thanks,' I replied curtly. Right away I knew immediately where it was all going. I wanted to leave. Disappointment flooded over me and I suddenly thought of my mother.

'Sit down, Sofia, and let's have a chat,' he said, looking me up and down. 'What are you into?' he continued, looking at my cleavage.

'Well I'd like to try out Bollywood, but back home I've got my own TV show,' I said, speaking quickly and stumbling over my words.

He carried on staring at my body, and I found myself pulling the collar on my blouse tightly around my neck.

'I've sung in a number of girl bands. I'm an all-round performer really, but my goal is to act in films.'

'I meant what are you into *sexually*,' he said, laughing, his chin wobbling from side to side. 'Maybe we can spend the evening together and find out what you really want to do? I'm sure we can come to some arrangement so that I can help you with your aim.'

His bloodshot brown eyes bore into me and I felt sick. It was time to leave. I didn't care how big this guy was in Bollywood, or what part he might have given me – there was no way I would ever prostitute myself like that. My skin crawled and I sat frozen rigid, paralysed by the situation. Thoughts of my mother started to fly into my mind – I wanted her to come and protect me.

Sitting there, I realised that this sleazy world was the one my mother knew about and wanted to protect me from, and within moments I had stood up and walked out of the room. I knew that Ricky was at a safe distance outside and was relieved to see him. We wasted no time in leaving the house.

But, from this negative experience, I gained something so positive – a clearer understanding about where my mother's fears were founded. It made me realise where my mother's principles about the performance industry being cheap had come from. All of a sudden, I understood that what she had done had been born out of the fear of something like this happening to me. This knowledge gave me the strength to try to work towards a reconciliation between us. To an outsider, what she'd done to me would seem so extreme, but I wanted to try to forgive her, especially now I understood her more fully.

I felt so sad as Ricky and I travelled home in the rickshaw. I felt sad for my mother because I hadn't understood her back in Brighton, and I felt sad because what had just happened seemed to mark the end of my Bollywood dream. But, as we drove through the dusty streets of Bombay, I began to feel better – I knew that my Bollywood dream wasn't ever to happen, but seeing my mother again had become a strong possibility, and that was a good thing.

After the final selection by the *Bollywood Star* judges I came fourth. I didn't care because I'd found something much more important on my journey, plus managing to get into the final had been great for me anyway. The film in which the winner would star was to be called *Nasar*. Rupak won the part and I was happy for her, but at the same time I was disappointed, as she had a very minor role and was certainly not portrayed as a Bollywood star.

When I came back to the UK and watched the show, I couldn't stop crying. I felt happy that I'd started to understand my mother, and that her attitudes had been born out of her desire to protect me. I was also glad that I'd learned about the dark side of the industry.

But I was also shocked – I didn't recognise myself; this was not the Sofia I thought I was. There were parts that were hugely edited to make me look like a somewhat iffy person, but I understood that – that's the nature of these kinds of shows. It was something else that I saw. I saw a woman who still had a lot to resolve in her life. From seeing myself on TV, I knew I needed to find a part of me that was well and truly missing. I needed my mother's love.

CHAPTER NINETEEN

TIMOTEI GIRL

A sadness had begun to creep up on me, but not because I wasn't getting any work or because I'd come fourth in the show. I just suddenly felt lost and confused. I was slipping into a personal low.

After India, I noticed that thoughts about my mother were frequently seeping into my mind. I wanted her with me again. Although the incident in the director's office had made seeking a resolution with her more pressing for me, when I got home I didn't know how to go about it. I contemplated meeting her, but as the days passed I feared that she might reject me.

Another worry was that I was approaching 30 and suddenly wanted to find stability in my personal life. Yes, I was coping, and had been enjoying my freedom and independence but, since I'd run away from home, I'd always lived day by day and was often alone. For many years, I'd relied on fate and friendships and being spontaneous and open-minded. Trusting God had also helped me survive.

For a long time, this way of living had worked wonderfully well, and I'd been happy, but as I began maturing I realised it was not enough – something was missing. I knew I had to make my mind up about seeing my mother and perhaps even find a companion too.

My agent Jennifer was really understanding during this time. She knew all about my past and understood exactly what I was going through. She was still putting me up for different jobs while trying to keep me on track.

'You've got the profile now,' she would say reassuringly, 'so I can send you to bigger auditions. This is just the beginning for you. There are always going to be highs and lows, Sofia. This business is unpredictable, but you can't give up now. There's so much more out there for you to do. I know it's hard because you've only yourself to rely on, but you've always managed everything so brilliantly. You're not alone.'

I told her I wasn't giving up, but that I just needed some space to think about my future. I explained that I needed to focus on my personal life. It had finally dawned on me how hard a lot of things had been and I was exhausted. She was great about it all. After a few serious chats over several weeks, Jennifer and I decided that I really needed some light relief for a few months. Taking the pressure off at work would give me space to resolve my personal dilemmas, we hoped.

I knew the money that I could make from shooting TV commercials would be good, plus I wouldn't have to learn long scripts and spend too much time away from my flat. Most of the commercials were in London, and were often day shoots that paid really well. Jennifer and I agreed to focus on that area for the time being. TV commercials would add a new string to my bow, too.

My first opportunity to do a TV advert was for Doritos crisps with TV presenter Vernon Kay. The advert was for their Spicy Tandoori line and they wanted me because of my Asian looks. I knew the production team had seen me on *Bollywood Star*, and I felt I'd have a good chance. I was excited and upbeat about the prospect of the ad, but to my dismay they then turned me down before I'd even been to the casting.

Jennifer let me know I hadn't got the part, and, feeling slightly dejected, I went into the kitchen to make myself a cup of tea. I don't know what came over me but, as I sat looking out on to the garden, I decided that I'd go for the casting anyway! I suppose my gut instinct told me to do so, even though I knew there'd be a risk of upsetting Jennifer and her cancelling our contract. I knew there was a risk of feeling worse if I was rejected again, but it was a risk I was prepared to take.

I hadn't even seen the audition brief, so I knew that turning up would be a complete and utter gamble. Even so, I put my thinking cap on and made sure that I fitted what I hoped they wanted. Jennifer had told me that they said I wasn't glamorous enough in the photo she'd sent them, so on the day of the casting I dressed up sexily and put on an East-meets-West-inspired outfit. I headed over to Marylebone, praying that they'd like me when they saw me in the flesh.

I arrived at the studio nervous, but determined to prove them wrong. 'You're not on the list,' the director barked at me, as I stood in front of the panel in my vibrant outfit.

'Well, I got a call from my agent, so I don't know what the mix-up could've been,' I said unashamedly fearing that they would suss me out. I had a feeling, though, that, once they saw me perform, they would love me. Something inside me just would not let this one go. I had told a white lie, but I had a good feeling about it.

'OK,' he snapped, 'seeing as you're here, let's see what you can do.'

He handed me the script and I waited for them to get the camera and lights ready. I read through the lines carefully, desperate to get them right so that I could make some sort of an impact. When I finally looked up and saw everyone waiting for me to start, I had a thousand butterflies in my stomach. But, when I stood in front of the director and began the casting, the fluttering quickly disappeared.

I felt great when I'd finished. I knew that I'd done a really good job. I also knew that they liked me because the director was suddenly smiling. Then he asked me if and when I was available.

'We're sorry for the mix-up,' he said. 'We like you. Your look is perfect. But you'll have to wait until we've decided. The audition was good so your agent will get a call.'

I felt really positive about the casting, but I wasn't sure that I'd got it. I'd been in so many situations where the casting director had loved me, but I'd never heard back. Then there was the issue of my showing up unannounced. Whatever the outcome would be, I had to make the call to Jennifer in the meantime and explain what I'd done.

'To be honest, I'm a bit upset,' said Jennifer when I told her what I'd done. 'I know what you're going through right now, but it'll make me look unprofessional. But what's done is done, so let's see.'

I knew that Jennifer was angry with me for going behind her back, but I felt glad that she hadn't gone as far as to cancel our agreement. I just prayed that something positive would come out of it all and that our relationship wouldn't be affected by my actions.

Jennifer called me back the next day. I'd got the job! I was ecstatic and so relieved, mainly because I hadn't let Jennifer down. 'I've got the contract and they want to start filming you in two weeks,' she explained. 'But next time let me know before you decide to do things on your own, Sofia. I know you're out of sorts at the moment but we need to continue to be level headed about business things.'

Jennifer was clear about her feelings, but I was glad that I'd done her proud at the casting. I still couldn't believe that I'd actually got the job. Maybe it was because I was feeling shaky and unsure about my personal life. Even when I turned up on set on the day, I thought one of the crew would tap me on the shoulder, tell me that they'd got the wrong girl and send me home. But they didn't, and my first TV commercial went really well.

The shoot was at Stansted Airport and we had to start filming really early because everyone had to go through so many security checks. I noticed that there were loads of extras waiting around and I felt very lucky because I was the lead. Then Vernon came out and we all got stuck in. It was a fun, sexy commercial and Vernon was really nice to work with. I laughed a lot because he kept messing up his lines and I kept prompting him. He'd joke about me being a 'clever clogs' and then he'd wink at me cheekily. The day went so quickly because Vernon was so much fun to be around. It was also fantastic seeing the ad on TV because I felt really proud.

After that, I did another TV advert for Lloyds Bank. Before the casting, Jennifer primed me about the role. I needed to look demure and serene and just smile at the camera – it was more a case of interacting well with the camera than having to do any sort of dialogue. When I arrived at the audition studio, I noticed that every other actress was white Caucasian and I felt at a loss.

'Have I come to the right casting?' I asked the director during the lunch break.

'Of course,' he said. 'You'll be fine. You'll be called up after lunch because there's a delay.'

Finally, it was my turn. I'd spent the morning watching all the other girls do their auditions, so I knew that all I had to do was to smile broadly and relax as I pretended to lead a beautiful black horse. I walked up and stood in front of the huge white backdrop. I didn't even have time to breathe before the cameras started to roll, so I just gave the camera a huge smile and carefully and calmly pretended to lead the horse. It was over so quickly, but I did it and must have done it well because my agent called the next day and said I'd got the job.

The next week I was shooting in Pinewood Studios. Once again it was an early start, and I was on set and fully made up before sunrise. It was a long day, but I loved every minute of it. Again, it was really satisfying seeing the ad on TV, especially because at the beginning my head filled the TV screen. What made this ad even more special to me was that Asian girls aren't normally cast in these types of ads. The producers wanted a woman who looked like she could be from anywhere and had a natural camera presence, and I fitted the bill.

The same year I shot an advert for Timotei shampoo. Timotei adverts normally featured Caucasian women with flowing blonde hair, so getting this gig was a real coup for me. The great thing was that the producers approached my agent saying they wanted me to audition, so when I got to the casting they were only seeing a few other girls, which made me feel really confident. 'I'm so glad you've made it, Sofia. You're early which is great. I've been trying to get you for some time for this audition,' the director said warmly.

I was thrilled when she told me I was definitely the best girl they'd seen. To top it off, she said that I'd got the job.

The Timotei advert was a short film that we shot over the next week at different locations in London. First off, we shot in a huge mansion in Surrey, and then we moved to other places such as Kew Gardens to film some exterior shots. The ad was shot very naturally – I was told to simply wash my hair every morning and turn up as I was. I had always imagined that, in commercials like this, the hair would have to be primed to perfection, but there was no hairdresser to make my hair look different, so I just put a brush through it and was ready. The schedule was tight that week. To make sure we got everything done, we started each day at dawn. That way, we managed to wrap up every day before the dark set in.

I'd chosen to spend time shooting TV commercials so that I could have some space to think, but it was a particular event at work that led to me making an important decision.

There was a little girl called Pearl who played my daughter in the ad. She was like a little angel and clearly loved the work. Midway through the week, I remember thinking how Pearl seemed so happy performing, and that she was young and had the world at her feet. Her youthful happiness and passion really struck me and it made me think of my past. Pearl's mother would brush her hair so that it looked perfect, and they'd sit there together laughing and joking. I remembered how my mum used to brush my hair some mornings. I would sit on the floor with my back towards her and she would plait it, ready for school. My heart ached as I watched Pearl's mother and helped me decide what I needed to do about my relationship with my mother.

The weekend after we finished shooting, I sat down and thought about how I felt. *Bollywood Star* and working with Pearl had both been quite emotional for me. I'd looked after myself for so long now that I'd forgotten what a mother/daughter relationship could really be like. I wanted to have a mother again.

For years, I had buried the need to have a mother and banished thoughts of her from my mind, but I had become desperate to get her back. After spending time with Pearl, I knew that I still had it within me to make one final try with Mum, even at the risk of rejection. I felt brave and sure enough to take the step.

By that time, my mother and father had separated and my mother had bought her own house. It had got to the point where she only came out of her bedroom to eat and wash. Eventually, my mother took control of her life, found work in a factory and saved up enough money to buy her own home. My sister Saira had helped my mother buy her house and had moved her out of our family home. On 12 June 1998, Saira had walked into the house on Northcote Road and, in front of my father, had helped my mother pack and move out.

I hadn't spoken to my father for years, and to this day we don't speak. He has tried to talk to me on the phone on many occasions, but I always hang up as soon as I hear his voice.

I thought that my sister Saira might be able to help me arrange a meeting with my mother. Saira had a very happy family by then. She had a husband, Ghulam Gos, and two little kids, Hunnah and Hamza, who I'd chatted to on the phone a few times. As well as wanting to see them and to get to know them, I assumed doing so might naturally bring me closer to my mother.

I phoned Saira one Saturday and asked if I could pick up the kids that afternoon and take them to the park. 'They're at Mum's new house,' said Saira. 'If you park up the road and toot your horn, they'll know to come out. That way you don't have to see Mum and vice versa.'

I did as she suggested, and every Saturday after that I travelled down to Gravesend, parked my car 15 metres up the road and beeped my horn so the kids would hear me. They'd run out of the house and we'd head off to the park together. They were always smiling when they saw me, which made me happy because those moments made me feel like I had a new little family.

One Saturday, Hunnah climbed into the car and said that my mother wanted to see me. It was all that I'd hoped for – I felt great.

'What? Now?' I said, flustered.

'Yes, Nanny said you could come in.'

I was shocked and asked her again and again if she was sure. She insisted that she was.

'Hold on,' I said. 'I need to call Saira and double check.' I was worried that Hunnah might have got it wrong. If she was right I was worried that my mother was about to shout at and reject me again, and I would not be able to handle that. I called Saira and told her my worries.

'It's fine,' said Saira. 'Just go and say Salam, and take it from there. Take it easy.'

'OK,' I said, 'I'll go. But please be on the other end of the phone in case it all goes wrong. Promise?'

'Promise. But don't worry – it'll be fine.'

I had made the decision. It was time to face my mother again.

I held Hunnah's hand tightly. We walked towards my mother's front door. I could feel my heart beating faster as we approached the little terraced house. I knocked on the front door, and the next thing I knew my mother was facing me. It was so strange standing there in front of her on the doorstep. It had been so long.

Her eyes seemed smaller – a little older and tired – and her hair had turned white, but she was still the same otherwise, although a bit less stressed. Time froze for a few moments, and I simply kept looking at her – even though I recognised her as my mother, I no longer knew her, or what she might say.

There was no big hug, no 'I love you' or 'I missed you', but there was a 'Hello, Sofia,' and those two words were more than enough for me.

'Come in. Do you want some tea?' my mother then asked me calmly.

'Yes, thank you,' I replied, suddenly feeling like a little girl again.

As I stepped inside, I was half expecting my world to crash on top of me again or for her to hurt me again. Neither happened.

My heart filled with joy as I journeyed through my mother's house and into the living room. The room was tidy, pretty and small, and in my father's absence it clearly reflected her personality. There was a lot of Islamic art around the house and ornaments on the mantelpiece. When I sat down on her couch and looked around, my heart skipped a beat: there was a picture of me on the wall!

I recognised the picture of my grandfather and me straight away because it had been taken when he had come to England many years before, when I was a child. There were various religious plaques hanging next to it, but the picture of me smiling up at my grandfather was without doubt central to the whole room. I looked away from the picture when my mother came in with a cup of tea. The next few hours were filled with small talk, but seeing the picture and being with my mother again made me feel great love towards her – I knew that, although she'd left me a decade ago on Brighton pier, my mother had kept me safely in her heart and home all along.

We didn't talk about my career, my father or why we'd been apart for so long. It was as if we were both avoiding those topics and wanted to feel like we'd never been apart. We were happy just to be together and drink our tea in the peace and quiet of her humble living room. I didn't want a painful reunion where we rehashed how I'd upset her, how she'd misunderstood me (and I her), and neither did she. For me, it was just a relief that she'd welcomed me into her home again. Because of that offering of peace, I felt nothing but happiness.

Before I left her living room that day, I glanced over at the picture of me in its telling place in the middle of wall, and I began to forgive my mother for everything.

After the meeting, I began phoning Mum every couple of weeks and went round to see her from time to time. Like a growing tree, we found our roots, and the branches are still growing. Sometimes a little blossom appears and someday that tree will hopefully bear fruit. The most important thing is that we have a relationship again.

After my mother bought her own house, my parents divorced and my father met a married woman who he is still with. They have since had a child together. I also found out that he had another child with a woman who had shared the house with my parents when my mother first came to the UK. I haven't met these two siblings.

Mum and I had a conversation recently where she told me that she feels down sometimes and doesn't know how to show what she's feeling inside.

'Why don't you try saying "I love you" to your kids?' I said, trying to help. 'I know we're adults, but just those words make a huge amount of difference.'

'Well, you all know that anyway, and it's not something I was brought up to do,' she said quietly.

I understood what she meant, but I wanted to try to help her break away from her past.

'Try it, Mum,' I said gently. 'It makes people feel warm and special. Just three very small but powerful words.'

I was surprised that day because we were on the phone for an hour and it seemed as if she was actually listening to me and getting something out of our conversation. My mother's priority was never love, but I couldn't hold it against her for not knowing any better. Her priority had been surviving the treatment my father handed out to her and feeding her family. I knew that my mother had the strength within her to learn and change.

Three days later, I was at my desk when the phone rang. It was my mother.

'Hi, Sofia,' she said. 'How are you?'

'Good, Mum, just working away,' I replied.

'I wanted to tell you something,' she began. I could hear a certain shyness in her voice. 'I do love you. I really do. Do you feel better now?'

I never thought in a million years that I'd hear my own mother saying those words to me.

'Yes, Mum,' I said with tears in my eyes. 'I feel really special. Thank you. Thank you so much.'

CHAPTER TWENTY

PLAY BOYS

During my time on *Sorted*, and when making the TV commercials, I became really interested in fashion. Making contact with my mother and finding peace and forgiveness freed up my senses and made me want to experiment with clothes even more. I felt more and more creative, and whatever I wore became an extension of who and what I was. Having fun with fashion also reflected the deep-rooted sense of fun that's within me. Being fashionable also boosted my self-confidence and femininity. And, because stars such as Mariah Carey had complimented me on my style, I realised that I had a natural eye for clothes.

After meeting Mariah, I constantly kept my eye out for inspiration wherever I went. I'd trawl through glossy fashion magazines, wander through all the vibrant, bohemian street markets in London, and people-watch when I went out in the West End and Chelsea. Eventually, it was my edgy sense of style and yearning to show off my femininity that catapulted me on to the pages of *Playboy* magazine. I became the first ever British Asian to be featured in its pages.

In November 2005, I made an outfit for the British premiere of a film called *Get Rich or Die Trying*, with American rapper 50 Cent playing the lead. It was a blue, Asian-styled little skirt and top, and the paparazzi went completely crazy when I stepped out of the car and on to the red carpet that night. I was so overwhelmed, and the next day my photos were plastered all over the Internet.

When my old boss at Zee TV called me up and congratulated me, I knew then that I was on to a good thing. He said he'd been contacted by press from all over the world asking questions about me. Accordingly, I started concentrating on my styling more in the hope that one of my outfits might eventually be spotted by someone special, and that someday I might go on to make clothes and have my own label.

It was when I attended the premiere for *The Interpreter* that my dreams came true. Again, I had created my own outfit and when I strolled up the red carpet I felt awesome. I'd designed a low-cut, black backless dress that fell to the base of my spine. It was quite daring but it did the trick and the paparazzi suddenly had me doing all sorts of poses in front of them. Amazingly, that particular dress inspired other designers across the world, and journalists wrote that I'd outshone Nicole Kidman at the premiere. Even more amazing was that wearing that dress led to my appearing in *Playboy* magazine.

I never thought that a magazine like *Playboy* would feature someone like me – I didn't think my figure was quite what they would be looking for and I'd never heard of any Asians appearing in *Playboy*. But one of my fans in America contacted me wanting to know where I bought my blue '50 Cent dress'. He told me that he'd seen the photograph of me wearing the dress in the American edition of *Playboy*, and sent me the article, where they'd run three pictures of me from various premieres. When I saw myself in the August 2006 edition, I was astounded to find that they had run a whole feature on my bottom – they said that it was amazing! What's more, it made sure that I was finally happy with my bum!

After the *Playboy* feature, I felt increasingly at ease with who I was and what I was becoming. I knew that I was daring, particularly as an Asian woman, but being *able* to be daring was so refreshing for me. I wanted to push the boundaries even further, so I began attending high-profile fashion events in London – at these events I knew I would be able to show off my sense of style even more.

The first big fashion event I ever attended was Fashion Rocks at the Royal Albert Hall. It is a prestigious annual event where top designers from around the world show off their latest designs. Supermodels parade down the runway as a well-known rock or pop band plays. That night, the guests included Naomi Campbell, Claudia Schiffer and Yasmin Le Bon, and Beyonce, Robbie Williams, Bjork, Jay Kay, Grace Jones and Duran Duran all performed.

That night I was wearing a dress that had been made by a student. I'd chosen it because it really told a story about me. The student was an up-and-coming designer hoping to make her mark on the world. I'd seen her work at a fashion show and contacted her directly to ask her to make me an outfit I'd show off for her at the party. Because I'd seen something in her, I wanted to give her a chance of making it. The outfit was a huge ra-ra skirt, which was fun and quirky, worn with a slinky sexy top. It had lines of gems on the back that zig-zagged down to the top of my hips, and made me feel like an Indian princess.

I had such fun that night chatting with Grace Jones, Kelis and Donatella Versace. Before I knew it, it was getting late and time to go. I went to collect my coat from the cloakroom, joining the queue of celebrities who were eager to get home.

'Who the f**k does she think she is?' shrieked a man from behind me. 'It's that Bjork pushing in again,' he added, laughing to himself.

I turned and saw it was Jay Kay – he was furiously trying to stop Bjork from jumping the queue. I laughed as I watched Bjork shrink away in fear and sidle off down the hallway. She started making frantic calls on her mobile, probably to ask someone else to collect her coat for her. Meanwhile, Jay Kay seemed to have forgotten about Bjork – now he was focusing his attention on me.

'What's your name?' he said. 'You look like an Indian princess in that gear.' It was odd that he'd thought the same thing as I had when I tried the outfit on.

We ended up exchanging numbers that night, and over time I discovered that Jay Kay was really cute and funny. 'Come down to The Manor,' Jay would say when he rang me every week. 'Lord Kay requests the pleasure of the Indian princess.'

I'd giggle back, and loved hanging out with him. I grew really fond of the eccentric and fun-loving singer, and always looked forward to his calls and funny text messages. The texts would come regularly and would always be funny and sexy. Sometimes he'd write things like

'Come to The Manor wearing sexy heels', but I'd laugh those texts off and he'd do the same. I know that I lapped up the attention that this warm, funny man was giving me. Everything was so comfortable between us, because neither of us had any expectations of the other – although his texts might have suggested otherwise, he never made me feel pressured into anything.

Sometimes Jay would come up to London and I'd see him at The Collection. The rest of the time we'd just phone or text. That winter Jay invited me to his 30th birthday party at The Manor. I decided to wear something understated, so I dressed in a tailored, fitted suit and heels and drove down to the country. I was pretty excited as I approached the party. The entrance to the house had huge wrought-iron gates across it, and a smartly dressed guard waved me in.

Jay had set up a huge marquee outside his mansion and there were a few security people milling about. I had been invited to the sit-down dinner, but I'd got lost on the drive down and knew that I had missed it. I was nervous about walking through the house alone and into the marquee – I didn't know anyone apart from Jay, and I wasn't sure if they were all still eating.

'Sofia! You made it!' I heard Jay shout from the other side of the marquee. 'We've finished eating but come and have drinks. There are fireworks later. I'm so glad you came!' He looked thrilled to see me.

It was a great party and, just as Jay had promised, there was an amazing fireworks display at the end of the night. I looked around me after the display and it hit me what a decadent party it really was. Beverley Knight sang happy birthday to Jay, and Geri Halliwell joined in.

I met up with Jay Kay a few times after that. He'd give me a call or I'd see him at various celebrity events. In the end, Jay just became a great friend. I knew that I still wasn't ready to get involved with a man.

I was offered my first feature film after meeting Jay Kay. I felt that everything in my life was finally falling into place. Gradually, everything that I'd ever hoped for *was* coming true! Although I still hadn't found love, I had a feeling that it wasn't that far away.

Finally, Sofia seemed at peace.

CHAPTER TWENTY-ONE
FILM STAR

My agent called to tell me that a director had contacted her. He wanted me to attend the casting for his film, *Exitz*, starring Malcolm McDowell.

'Can you sing opera, Sofia?' asked Jennifer hopefully.

I'd had some vocal training in the past and had attended my own singing classes, but I'd never sung opera, apart from in the shower!

'Not really, Jennifer,' I said, 'but I'd love to try. Would I be able to audition anyway and get some lessons beforehand?'

'Yes. They've asked for you so why don't you just try. It's next week though.'

I definitely didn't want to miss out on the opportunity to work alongside such a high-profile and respected star, and I knew my voice was strong enough. I decided that all I could do was my best. I decided not to take any lessons and instead just mimicked some songs from *Phantom of the Opera*.

The next week, I went along to the casting and confidently told the casting director I could sing opera before giving it my all.

'That was excellent, Miss Hayat,' said the director as he clapped my performance. 'You're exactly what we want. Your acting resume is good and your vocal tone and strength is perfect. We'll get in touch with your agent soon about start dates, and we look forward to working with you on set.'

'Thanks so much,' I replied.

I was filled with excitement and very relieved. It was hard not to jump for joy, but I kept my composure as I walked out of the audition room. Once outside, I called Jennifer and told her the great news: I'd got the part.

'Wow, that was a quick decision,' she exclaimed. 'They must've loved you! Well done, Sofia. You're really getting there.'

Her words meant so much, and what's more I agreed with her. I *was* getting somewhere, and it was a wonderful feeling.

Shooting began three weeks later. I played Beauty – as in *Beauty And The Beast* –and I was the star of the opera in the film. It felt ironic to be playing Beauty, considering I'd always been bullied for being ugly, and it said it all about how much things had changed for me. I had to lay down my vocal tracks first, so went to a recording studio for a couple of days and then started shooting in a country house.

Exitz has a fantastic plot about an illegal immigrant who is a computer buff. He creates a computer game that controls the other characters, but his real life becomes so interweaved with the game that the viewer is faced with the challenge of differentiating between fantasy and reality. Working with Malcolm was amazing. Although he was the most famous actor there, he was without doubt the most charming. He was flirtatious in a very gentlemanly way; he constantly made me laugh and he had this glint in his eye which made the shoot days even more interesting.

The days were long. Filming kicked off at 6am and finished around 8pm. It was hard work, but because I was a novice I was on a steep learning curve and it felt great. I picked everything up really quickly and one thing I learned was how to be patient. Scenes would have to be reshot from various angles or if there was any extraneous noise picked up by the microphones. Plus, if the make-up people noticed shiny patches on anyone's faces, they had to be retouched.

Soon after I'd finished *Exitz*, I managed to get a new agent. I still valued Jennifer, but I was moving forward so quickly that I needed someone bigger behind me. Around this time, I was offered a casting for a feature film by a famous Bollywood director called Vivek Agnihotri. I was sceptical about trying my hand in Bollywood, since I'd had that difficult experience with the director I met during *Bollywood Star*, and I felt that I was in a position to turn things down if I wanted to. In the back of my mind, I was also thinking about my next film project, *The Unforgettable*, which Jennifer had kindly secured for me, so I declined *Goal* and went on from there.

I was quite nervous when I went to the casting for *The Unforgettable* at Pinewood Studios. I knew that there would be talented actresses there including Sophiya Haque, who'd incidentally been a judge on *Bollywood*

Star. However, I did my best and got through the first casting. I was called back to do another reading later in the week. Even though I put so much effort into it, the reading didn't go very well and I really didn't think I'd got the part. I was relieved when it was over and decided that, if I wasn't successful, then at least I'd tried. I knew I'd reached a really good point in my acting career because I was getting auditions like that quite regularly and could finally start to plan ahead. I had actually thought that Sophiya Haque got the job and even sent her a text message to congratulate her.

So I was shocked when I got a call from Jennifer to say that I'd got the job. I was over the moon, and couldn't wait for the full script to arrive so that I could get stuck into learning my lines. The part would be my biggest yet, so I really needed to shut myself away in my flat for a good few weeks and focus on learning it. *The Unforgettable* was my first major film and, frankly, I was daunted by it all; but after the script had arrived and I'd gone over and over the lines I knew that I could pull it off perfectly. The scenes moved, challenged and excited me.

There were quite a few big names involved in the project, so I was quite nervous as I desperately didn't want to let anyone down. The leading actor was Raji James who had been in *East is East*, *Nina's Heavenly Delights* and *EastEnders*. I found out that the director of photography was a guy called WB Rao, who is hugely respected in Bollywood and has worked with some of the biggest stars in the industry including Amitabh Bachan.

A few months before I set off for Mauritius to make the film, I planned an intimate dinner at Cipriani restaurant in

Mayfair. I'd been hard at work learning the lines and wanted to thank my friends Federica Biti, Chris Hayes and Dawn for supporting me and just spend time relaxing with them before I jetted off. And I wanted to take them somewhere really special.

I love Cipriani because it has a filmic ambience that harks back to the days of Marilyn Monroe. It is very romantic, and has antique chandeliers and very attentive, impeccably dressed and handsome staff. They always seem like they have just stepped out of *Italian Vogue* (and the clientele are equally glamorous, of course!).

That night, I wore a blue Pucci dress. It was low cut at the front and figure-hugging in all the right places. I felt fantastic as we walked into the bar and were met with a glass of the famous Cipriani Bellini. We enjoyed our drinks before being shown to our table.

Once we had sat down, I noticed a man staring at me. It wasn't just a glance, but a long drawn-out stare. I tried to carry on focusing on my guests, but every time I looked up I couldn't help looking back at David Beckham – he looked so handsome. I could hardly believe that David Beckham was sitting about three metres away and staring at me. I found it quite funny at first, but the funniest thing was that David wasn't even making conversation with the man he was with.

Because David was staring so much, I began to give as good as I got and returned his gaze. I almost choked on my food when it finally arrived. At that point David smiled even more. I blushed and blushed.

'What's wrong, Sofia?' asked my friend Dawn.

She then turned and saw David looking at me. 'Oh my God, he's staring at you!' she exclaimed.

'What am I supposed to do?'

'Stare back!' she said, laughing.

I smiled at David again, and he smiled back.

After our main course, I went to the ladies. I had to take a deep breath as I crossed the restaurant – I knew that David's eyes were following me. I was startled when I came out and drew an even deeper breath. David was standing directly in front of me. I froze and simply stared at him.

'You're far more sexy in real life,' I blurted, and then I blushed. I'd never said that sort of thing to a stranger before, and I wasn't sure what had come over me – I suppose I thought David Beckham should know how sexy he was! I didn't expect him to return the compliment, but he did, telling me he thought I was sexy too.

I stood there for a few seconds, speechless.

As David opened his mouth to speak again, Dawn appeared. 'We've finished dinner, Sofia. We've ordered the bill,' she said.

'Fine. I'm coming,' I said, still smiling at David. I then followed Dawn back to the table to wait for the bill. Five minutes later, David also returned to his table. When our bill came, I paid it quickly and we left.

I was papped when I left Cipriani, but all I could think about was how starstruck I'd been. I'd never felt that way when faced with a celebrity, and the intensity of the experience made me wonder if the time had finally come when I could be receptive and confident with men again. I'd wanted to flirt again, just like I'd done with Jay Kay, but more so. I was ready to take things further with someone. I still couldn't believe what I'd said to David, but I must have had a huge smile on my face – the paparazzi took one look at me flagging a cab on the pavement, and were soon busy clicking away.

Oddly, I was about to get on the tube a few days later when a few guys whistled at me. I turned and smiled, and then one of the train inspectors shouted across to me, 'That's a great smile,' he said. 'You'd be just David Beckham's type! You could have a guy like that if you wanted.'

'Thanks!' I laughed. As I took my seat on the tube, I remembered the days when I couldn't even turn my head when men whistled or smiled at me in the street, and now I was able to laugh with them so confidently.

One Sunday afternoon, Federica invited me out in Knightsbridge and mentioned that she was bringing along a friend. We met at Bardot on Walton Street, a plush bar frequented by many A-listers, bankers and businessmen.

'This is Fabrizio,' she said, smiling. Something about him made me nervous and my stomach fluttered as I held out my hand to this attractive, well-dressed, dark-haired man. I remember thinking that he had the most amazing smile and, even though I hadn't met him before, he seemed familiar to me.

That night, we drank cocktails and danced Salsa together, after which Fabrizio offered me a lift home. He seemed kind and unassuming and, after he kissed my cheek softly in the cab, we swapped numbers.

Four days later, Fabrizio called and invited me over for dinner at his house in Pimlico. I was so excited as I picked out what to wear. I decided on jeans and a white fitted top – nothing over the top, but sexy and chic.

When I got to his place, I was so nervous that I couldn't

bring myself to press the buzzer and ended up ringing Saira to get some sisterly support. We giggled on the phone about it and she helped me to overcome my nerves sufficiently to ring the bell. Saira and I still laugh about that call today because we both realised that my terrible nerves said it all. I must have really liked this man.

Fabrizio answered the door, his kind face smiling. He led me into a room which was filled with candles. I was overwhelmed – no one had ever done anything that romantic or thoughtful for me before.

'It looks beautiful,' I gasped.

Fabrizio cooked fillet steak and vegetables and we shared a bottle of good red wine. The flat looked on to the river so after dinner we sat and watched the stars glistening in the sky and the water light up beneath us. We were on the 12th floor so I could see the Millennium Wheel, Big Ben and thousands of apartment lights shining around us. When the kiss finally came, it was just how I'd imagined. Perfect.

Our first kiss was a beautiful moment and we often talk about it. But the best thing was that I opened up to Fabrizio that night. I didn't know him, yet I felt that I did and he felt the same way about me too. I told him about my past, my mother, Daphne... everything. And as I talked and talked, I looked over and there he was listening intently to every single word. No man had ever been there for me like that and I cherished his attention so entirely.

I loved Fabrizio that night and I still love him to this day.

Federica giggled when I told her that I'd spent the night talking and cuddling him, and that he didn't expect anything physical. She was so happy for me and she trusted my judgement. I knew my emotions so well by then and I knew that this man was the one. The chemistry and the mental connection. It was all so perfect.

Naturally, our relationship moved on very quickly. Fabrizio whisked me off skiing a few weeks later and showered me with love. When there were down moments and I felt frustrated in my work, Fabrizio was there by my side immediately. His hugs, smiles and warmth are what really get me through. He helps me forget the bad and his being there provides me with the good in my life.

A few months after we met, he told me that he loved me. It was after we'd first made love and I remember when he looked into my eyes and whispered the words to me I rushed into the bathroom, grinning from ear to ear and then punching the air shouting, 'Yes!'

However, I didn't tell him my feelings until about a month later. We'd flown to Thailand for a holiday and had joined Federica and her boyfriend on a private yacht. It was a magical trip and as we sailed around the islands we fell even further in love. One day we sailed to the island where Leonardo DiCaprio had filmed *The Beach* and I remember sitting on the white sand with Fabrizio alone. I took his hands, looked into his eyes and I knew that was the right moment so I told him exactly how I felt. We knew from that moment that we would be together forever.

In those first few months with Fabrizio, I learned so much about myself and my sexuality, that making love is more about allowing yourself to be vulnerable to really enjoy it. For the first time, sex was something beautiful, not dirty. I felt as though I'd finally been freed of the past abuse I had suffered. I was no longer afraid of sex.

I was so wrapped up in Fabrizio before I left that I was on cloud nine when I boarded the plane to Mauritius with Raji James and the rest of the cast. I'd wanted to spend all my time with Fabrizio before leaving, so now I needed to start putting my all into the script again. During the flight, I sat far away from the others and read and reread it. The scenes were heavy and involved and I wanted to be fully competent when we started work the next day. I pored over my lines and I was so captivated by my character, Padma, that in my mind I became her.

Padma was a glamorous character to play and there were a lot of meetings for me to go to with wardrobe, hair stylists and make-up. I quickly settled into my hotel room and was primed by the production assistant about life on the island, with particular focus on the climate and the food. I was told not to go out in the sun – they needed my skin to keep its colour and not go any darker in the sun, for continuity reasons. I was to be careful with what I ate outside of the hotel – they could not risk me getting ill from experimenting with the local cuisine. I was told to make sure I rested in between shoots because the shooting days would be up to 15 hours long, and the filming schedule was spread over two months. I assured the assistant I would do my very best, and I meant it.

Filming began early the next morning. I loved every minute of the work, although the love scene I had to shoot halfway through the first month was really challenging – I'd never even had a screen kiss at that point. In the build-up to the shoot, I kept psyching myself up by looking in the mirror and repeating a mantra to myself – 'I'm Padma. I'm in control.' I felt it would calm my nerves and keep me in character, and I was right. When the love scene came up, I flew through it, and the director was really pleased.

The film was about true passion, love and making love, and it was essential that I had a good understanding of those elements in order to play my part well. Until I met Fabrizio, my experiences with men had given me a tainted view of love and sex. Sex had harmed me as I went through my teens and twenties and I had abstained from it for a few years as I didn't want to have sex outside the context of a meaningful relationship. I was in a film where sex was a beautiful thing, and my character was in control, and clearly allowing herself to embrace it. I was able to communicate that on screen because I had finally felt good about sex with Fabrizio, and therefore understood the character I was playing. I'm thankful that, through both Fabrizio and my job, I finally let this beautiful and powerful part of me come out fully.

The other amazing thing about my time in Mauritius was that I managed to find real peace with my culture. Most of the film crew were Indian, Hindu or Muslim so I was suddenly back within a world that had shunned me and that I had questioned for so long. But, this time, I saw something very different. I saw Asians, including Muslims, working on a film that had a love scene in it. They had written and embraced this magnificent story of love. Everyone on the set came from the culture in which I had grown up, but this felt so different. It was free and unrestricted. The culture that I'd been brought up in had obviously been highly restrictive, but doing what I loved best with creative people from India really changed my views about the way I viewed my culture. I was surprised at how liberal it was. Finally, I didn't feel threatened or judged by it any more. I felt accepted. And all the while I was making a film!

Arsala Qureishi, the Indian Muslim scriptwriter, really inspired me. She was the first Muslim woman I met who was brave enough to do something like this and do it with her family's support. I remember how lucky I thought she was to have her mother and brother with her on set – they were so proud of her. The film was based on an episode from her life and she was brave to talk about it in this way and create something so powerful from it, and so fortunate to have her Muslim mother supporting her. This gave me further acceptance of who I was and what I did.

At one point we were filming during Ramadan, and I fasted and prayed rigorously for the first time in years. It was really strange yet so nourishing for me – for the first time in my life what I was doing as an actor reflected my culture and religion. I was fasting and praying and making a movie. It was surreal, but I found peace in Mauritius.

On the last night, I remember sitting by my hotel window and looking out on to the beautiful azure sea. I kissed the glittering diamond engagement ring that Fabrizio had given me the night before I left for Mauritius and watched the sky turn blood red in the setting sun. I knelt down on my prayer mat and said a prayer.

There are certain things that I have achieved in recent years of which I am particularly proud and which, when I think about them, remind me how far I have come and how hard I have worked to be doing what I do now.

In 2004, I was nominated by Croydon College students to be their guest of honour at their graduation ceremony. The year before the guest had been the designer Yves

Rocher so it was a real surprise and a real honour when they asked me! I was thrilled that the students saw me as someone who could inspire them. I was so proud when I made my speech, telling them that it is possible for your dreams to be realised, even when those around you might not believe in what you are doing.

Another vote of confidence came from the Gurkhas, who voted for me to be the celebrity to go and entertain them. I sang all sorts of songs for them including Bollywood songs and my own numbers, which are mostly an East/West fusion. My visit turned into a ten-day tour and it was an amazing experience. I felt really humbled when I learned of the dangers that they face and I continue to support them.

But it was in December 2007 that one of my dearest dreams came true when I sang solo at The Royal Albert Hall in front of thousands of people. A woman who had seen some of my work on television rang me to ask if I would host a concert to raise money for the Pakistani Earthquake Appeal. I agreed but only on the condition that I could sing too. Luckily for me, she agreed! The concert was only 48 hours away, so I didn't have long to prepare. I sifted through songs that I had written and recorded, before finally settling on an upbeat one called 'Choley'.

While I was planning other details such as what I would wear and how I would perform the dance to accompany my song, my phone rang. It was my sister, Saira, with tragic news. One of my extended family, Mozma, was in hospital. She was just 22 years old and had been diagnosed with cancer three months earlier. She didn't have long left to live.

I hurried to the hospital and found her room, where many relatives were praying at her bedside. It was the first time many of them had seen me for years. Mozma looked terrible and it was obvious that she didn't have much time left. I stayed for a few hours and prayed as I held her hand.

When I got home, I didn't feel in the mood for dancing and jumping around on stage. I began to think about the people who would be coming to the concert, and the people they were raising money for. I thought about Mozma and her illness and suddenly felt compelled to write.

It took me only two hours to write 'One More Day', a song about appreciating those around you who love you. Sadly, Mozma passed away the next morning but I had my song ready for her and I put my heart and soul into the night ahead.

I worked tirelessly through the rehearsals with a guitarist called Franck and we perfected everything in just three hours. Just 48 hours after I'd got the call to host the night, I was standing on stage ready to sing. As I stared out at the audience my body trembled. I couldn't see their faces but they were clearly there waiting for me to start. The Albert Hall was deadly silent but I sang my heart out and the applause then shook the entire concert hall. I can honestly say that was the most amazing day of my life and, as I ran to the dressing room, I was met by a BBC crew who wanted to interview me.

The *Independent* described my song as 'a hit' and that was so rewarding for me. I had seen Beyonce sing there a few years before I'd stood on that very same stage. As I had sat there in the audience, I remembered thinking to myself how amazing it would be to stand up there and sing as she was doing. And just a few years later I was there, performing my solo track on the very same stage! It was amazing.

Today, professionally, I am looking forward to my two film releases in 2009 (*The Unforgettable* and *Cash and Curry*). I'm also throwing all my creativity into a film script that is titled *I Don't Want To Marry Shah Ruck Khan*. We hope to start filming towards the end of next year. I'm also singing and writing to my heart's content and, although I don't have a major record deal, you never know!

On the personal front, Fabrizio and I are making plans to marry with Federica as my bridesmaid (of course!). In fact, my family life couldn't be more perfect right now given that there is so much excitement and change ahead of me. I see my mother quite often and she even sends me birthday cards. I send her Mother's Day cards which is fantastic because, after hating Mother's Day for so many years, now I can enjoy it. I know that she couldn't be the mother I needed in the past, but I have forgiven her and she has forgiven me. What matters to me most is now and today we are both thriving in our new relationship with one another which we know is an amazing feat in itself. I secretly think, however, that my mother feels proud of what I have achieved to date. She'd never say it but I can see it in her eyes when she greets me or says goodbye.

My sister Saira has a beautiful family, with four stunning children. These blessed children have the love and freedom that they deserve and we often spend time together. I am also slowly getting closer to my other siblings, Abdul Wajid (who also has an amazing family) and Tahira. We three are taking steps to become a family unit once again and thankfully, slowly but surely, we are getting there.

Every New Year's Eve, I still think about Arissa. I make a point of sitting in my study on that evening, and I look out over the Downs with her in my mind. I wonder perhaps if she may be alive and well. It's a small hope, but I keep it there during those moments and it helps – we need to keep hope alive in our lives.

I hope that other women out there, like Arissa, who are trapped within the same awful predicament can find courage and eventually find their exit. Many, unfortunately, may never find it. If they fail (and I pray that they won't), then there is one thing that I hope they can at least learn along the way – and that is to always love themselves and that each and every one of us is important no matter what we are and where we are in the world.

I know that perhaps if I'd looked in the mirror as a child and said, 'I'm important,' then my childhood might have been less painful. It's never too late to follow a dream and to believe in yourself. It's never too late to start again. You can become anything you choose to become. That first day in Brighton, when I looked down from the pier at the vast, open and thriving sea, I saw freedom in all its swirling splendour for the first time. We are all children of the universe and every one of us deserves to be free and happy.